Windows for the Journey

Prose, Prayers, and Poems for the Daily Walk

Wallace W. Horton

Foreword by Carla Waterman

© 2022
Published in the United States by Nurturing Faith, Macon, GA.
Nurturing Faith is a book imprint of Good Faith Media (goodfaithmedia.org).

Library of Congress Cataloging-in-Publication Data is available.

ISBN: 978-1-63528-214-6
All rights reserved. Printed in the United States of America.

Unless otherwise indicated, all scripture citations come from the
New Revised Standard Version.

Dedication

To Joan:
You have been walking with me on our journey
For more than 51 years.
From the Heartland, to the West Coast, to the East Coast,
You have served with me in ministry in five wonderful congregations.
Through every part of our walk together
You have loved me, inspired me, guided me, and supported me.
You have been my partner in life, a mother to Rebecca and David,
And a grandmother to Esther, Grace, Mackenzie, and Mabel.
You have shared your faith and lived God's love.
You have shown me how to walk with Jesus.

"Wallace Horton's sequel to his insightful and refreshing *Windows on Worship* provides a delightful diversity of perspectives for the Christian life. The reader will find this collection to be very beneficial. The sections of prose, prayers, and poems are readable, relatable, and rich—enhanced with personal stories, Scripture, and hymn quotations. This small volume is perfect for personal and small group encouragement and inspiration. Open the windows of your soul to enjoy the fresh spiritual breezes."

—Robert Myers, D.W.S.
General Editor, Webber Institute Books

"Wallace Horton opens windows along the journey of life from his personal experiences, truths of Holy Scripture, and inspiring hymns, and from meaningful prose, prayers, and poems he has written. These are insightful views that are eye-opening, thought-provoking, soul-stirring, and faith-strengthening. This book is a journey worth taking."

—Paul Devantier, M. Div.
Speaker, *By the Way* Radio Ministry

"Wallace Horton's *Windows for the Journey* are 'real life' devotions, prayers, and poems written out of this author's personal journey with Jesus. Even though our journeys take us through surprises, rough roads, and vast seas, Dr. Horton reminds us that we are not alone on this journey, and that God is in the 'rescue business.'"

—Andy Lissy, M. Div.
Pastor, Living Savior Lutheran Church, Fairfax Station, Va.

"'Journey' is an apt word for Wallace Horton's book of devotions, prayers, and poetry. Personal stories, Scripture, beloved hymn quotations, and original prayers and poems are woven into a sojourn of reflection, petition, and praise—an encouragement for worship, personal and corporate. There is a sense both of affirmation of Christ's finished work for us and of being 'on the way'—leaning into and reflecting on our calling as Christians and servant leaders. Every page is an invitation to walk alongside and deepen our vision of Jesus."

—Linda Borecki, D.W.S.
Editor, Association of Lutheran Church Musicians, *In Tempo*

Contents

Foreword ix
Acknowledgments xi
Introduction xiii

Part 1

Prose for the Daily Walk 1
   This Is the Day 2
   The Seasons of Life 3
   Counting the Days 4
   Knowing the Way 5
   Faith Walking 6
   Following the Truth 7
   Walking in God's Call 8
   Praying When No One Is Watching 9
   Taking Care of God's Gifts 10
   Always Keep on Singing 11
   Recognizing God's Vision 12
   The "Eyes" Have It 13
   The Gift of "Do-Overs" 14
   Temptations: We All Have Them 15
   Obeying God's Voice 16
   Where Are Your Thoughts? 17
   Let God Love You 18
   The Greatest Thing 19
   Unexpected Suprises 20
   Never Far Away 21
   Wide Seas, Small Boats 22
   Winners and Losers 23
   Living in the Clouds 24
   The Vicissitudes of Life 25
   Words of Invitation 26
   A New Beginning 27
   Givers of Peace 28
   Imitating God 29

Part 2

Prayers for the Daily Walk 31
   ...for the start of a new week 32
   ...for the beginning of the day 33
   ...for the middle of the day 34
   ...for the end of the day 35
   ...for strengthening my prayer time 36

...for a deeper relationship with God.. 37
...for the Spirit 38
...for my service to God 39
...for times of learning how to pray 40
...for seeking guidance and direction... 41
...for God's mercy 42
...for times of discouragement.. 43
...for God's forgiveness to me and others... 44
...for times of thanksgiving 45
...for dealing with relationships.. 46
...for times of unexpected testing 47
...for discernment in a time of transition... 48
...for facing an unexpected medical diagnosis.................................... 49
...for dealing with the death of a loved one 50
...for the birth of a child or grandchild.. 51
...for God's benefits to me.. 52
...for my child 53
...for times when life isn't fair.. 54
...for protection against the devil.. 55
...for God-pleasing decisions 56
...for trusting God's will 57
...for being a "voice" for God... 58

Part 3
Poems for the Daily Walk...59
   We Run the Race 60
   Holy Hearts, Holy Minds 61
   Delight Yourself, Commit Your Way 62
   Walking Away.. 63
   When to Leave 64
   When God Says "Go" 65
   New Beginnings 66
   My Time on Earth 67
   O Morning Sun 68
   A Lasting Friendship... 69
   When Others Let You Down 70
   The People of the Lord 71
   Counting the Cost... 72
   The Mind of Christ 73
   My Lord and God 74

Notes 75
Scripture Index.. 77

Foreword

I met Wallace Horton nearly 20 years ago at the Robert E. Webber Institute for Worship Studies. He was a student in a memorable class of passionate, theologically astute church musicians. My partner, Rev. Dr. Reggie Kidd, and I found their class to be that kind of challenging joy that compose the best doctoral classes. Later, I had the privilege of leading a retreat at Dr. Horton's church with one of his doctoral cohort members, Dr. Linda Borecki. It, too, was a memorable time of spiritual deepening for us all.

From reading *Windows for the Journey: Prose, Prayers, and Poems for the Daily Walk*, I am aware that this is a lifetime work. Dr. Horton couldn't have written it when he was 30, nor could he have composed it in the last year. The themes range from birth to death, to the surprising work of God and the shocking distractions of the enemy, from the joys of everyday praise to knowing when it is time to leave a community. This book holds "windows" from many different moments throughout Wallace's life.

Because it is a lifetime work, there are several good ways to read it. First, read it as the faithful testimony of a long journey of faith. Just as Dr. Horton observed his grandfather and his father pray, observe him through these windows. Glimpse his questions, and the answers he hears from God. Appreciate the reflective prose, the prayers that pour from his soul, and the poems that capture his honest engagement with God on one hand and with life on the other.

Second, read it to discover the friends he has made with books and hymns along the way. His book list and his hymn selections are good windows to look through in discovering some jewels of the Christian life, for example this one:

> Come my soul, with ev'ry care,
> Jesus loves to answer prayer;
> He himself has bid thee pray,
> Therefore will not turn away.

I have always built my book list by observing what is being read by people I respect. Dr. Horton's list is peppered through his own prose and well worth paying attention to.

Finally, do not only read to observe and discover Wallace's windows. Look through them yourself. Let his windows inspire and lead you into your own prayers, your own ponderings of God's working in your life. Let *Windows for the Journey* be both a testament of one man's faithful journey and an inspiration for you on your own daily walk.

—Carla Waterman, Ph.D., Founding Professor
Robert E. Webber Institute for Worship Studies

Acknowledgments

The journeys that we embark upon are affected by many individuals, circumstances, and events in life. The same is true of the "windows" that are included in this book. The thoughts—prose, prayers, and poetry—have not been developed and shaped in isolation, but rather with the contributions and guidance of family members, friends, and colleagues over the years.

I am grateful to those who have walked part of their life's journey in the choirs and musical ensembles I have directed in the churches where I have served. Seeing their faith walks has been an inspiration to me in a variety of ministry settings.

The men of my Saturday morning Bible study group and my friends from the "Hour of Power" Bible study have provided wonderful examples of individuals who walk with the Lord each day. Thank you for sharing your challenges. You have provided me with pictures of various life situations, good and bad, and how, as a child of God, you respond.

Thank you to Carla Waterman, Bob Myers, Paul Devantier, Linda Borecki, and Andy Lissy for their friendship, support, and words of encouragement. Their shared wisdom has been a wonderful gift for me in the writing and completion of *Windows for the Journey*.

I am very appreciative of the support and work of my friends at Good Faith Media, especially Bruce Gourley for his guidance, Jackie Riley for her conscientious work in serving as the copy editor for this project, and Cally Chisholm for her design work.

My colleague and friend, Meghan Benson, has proofread the text numerous times and assisted me throughout the development of this book. Her contribution has been a true blessing to me. Thank you, Meghan.

Finally, thanks to all of you who will read *Windows for the Journey* as part of your daily walk with the Lord. May its words and thoughts strengthen you as you walk with Jesus.

Introduction

I've spent much of my adult life planning, writing, and thinking about the various aspects of Christian worship. The corporate gathering of the body of Christ; the presentation of the Word; the singing of "psalms, and hymns, and spiritual songs" (Col. 3:16); and the practices within the context of worship have helped to shape and guide my ministry. Those components are among some of the areas that I addressed in my previous book, *Windows on Worship*.

Windows for the Journey is, in a real sense, a sequel to my first book. While *Windows on Worship* gives much attention to the corporate worship experience, this book shares thoughts through prose, prayers, and poetry that can be used as a resource for personal worship and devotional times. While not intended to be pietistic in their application, some thoughts may help you to look inwardly at how to respond to God's prompting and calling. In responding to our Lord's words to us in our private times of worship, we are afforded the opportunity to strengthen and enhance the mission of the church and ministry to the world.

It is during our times of private worship and quiet meditation that we are often able to reflect upon our own journey through life and what the Lord might be saying to us. The answers to our questions are often given to us through the reading and study of Scripture. Other times those answers come to us by simply listening for and hearing God's voice. On some occasions, we can be helped and guided by the thoughts and writings of individuals who have shared some of the same experiences we might be having. I refer to these thoughts and writings as "windows."

In the construction industry, windows come in various shapes and sizes. Certain windows allow us to view people, objects, and panoramas. Some windows allow light to pass through them while other windows prevent the outside brightness from entering a space. There are colorful windows, frosted windows, stained glass windows, and clear windows. There may be windows that share a story while others remain neutral and simply serve as a barrier that protects us from the elements and other distractions. Different spaces and buildings require a variety of styles of windows. In short, different windows fulfill different needs and purposes.

Like construction windows, the windows in this book will have different shapes, sizes, and colors. As we each travel through our life-journey, we experience many different occurrences and episodes that span the entire spectrum of spiritual, emotional, relational, and physical conditions and challenges that can lift our spirits to great heights or, on the other hand, bring us to our knees. We can feel great joy and happiness on one day and be tested by pain and disappointment on the next day. During these various times, it can be helpful and encouraging to be able to meditate, pray, or reflect upon a thought, a prayer, or a verse that reminds us of God's love, support, and nearness. The Lord is always present during everything that our daily walk may reveal throughout our journey.

Windows for the Journey includes a variety of meditations, prayers, and poetic thoughts that address many of the circumstances and challenges that everyone faces or will face in life. There is no predetermined manner in how one might use this collection of writings. How you use this book will be determined by where you find yourself from day to day. You may read the same essay, poem, or prayer several days in a row. Perhaps it will be several days, or even weeks, between the reading of the same thought. However you choose to use this book, I encourage you to include the reading of Scripture, either of your own selection or the verse that accompanies a number of the meditations.

In writing *Windows for the Journey*, I have done so with the hope that you might identify with some of the thoughts and experiences I talk about, pray about, and respond to. Our loving Lord has specific and personal ways to come alongside of you as you travel the daily walk on your journey. I pray that your personal worship will be strengthened by the thoughts and prayers shared in these writings.

I appreciate that each of you may have experienced a variety of relationships with your own earthly parents that may influence your perspective of both motherhood and fatherhood. Throughout this book, I have written my "windows" using masculine pronouns for God. This practice has guided me all of my life and throughout my 50-plus years of ministry. God is neither male nor female, and loves all of his children with a perfect love.

May our wonderful God—Father, Son, and Holy Spirit—accompany you on your individual journey and daily walk, touching your spirit and heart as you let the Lord speak to you in the words of *Windows for the Journey*. God bless you.

Part 1

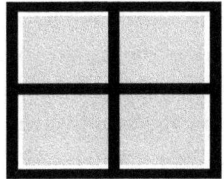

Prose for the Daily Walk

This Is the Day

This is the day that the LORD has made; let us rejoice and be glad in it.
(Ps. 118:24)

The words of Psalm 118:24 are a wonderful reminder that every day is a gift from God. As the Lord's child, you have many reasons to rejoice and be grateful. God's blessings are endless. Sometimes, however, we fail to recognize everything for which we should be thankful. Frankly, there are times when we are not in a "rejoicing" mood. Perhaps you are surrounded by overwhelming challenges. You may have unfinished responsibilities at home or at the office or at school. You know what you are facing and simply are not looking forward to addressing it. It might be dealing with a word that was spoken in haste or a relationship that needs to be repaired. Maybe it's a phone call you received from your doctor with a message you did not want to hear.

Perhaps you are concerned about a child who is still at home or even has "left the nest." It might be a decision you need to make that will be life-changing for you and your loved ones. There can be any number of situations that place you in lonely and dark places, that don't allow you to "rejoice and be glad in it."

How do you find your way out of those places of isolation and loneliness? How do you recapture that place where you *can* "rejoice and be glad in it"? Where do you turn? To whom do you listen? Where do you stand when you find yourself in those valleys that look so steep and forsaken?

It is during those times when you must "Be still, and know that I am God" (Ps. 46:10). Rather than talking and receiving word from well-intended sources, you need to be silent and listen for the voice of the Lord. You need to go into your quiet place and be just that—quiet.

For some of us, the discipline of listening does not come easily. We want answers. Often, we want to be the one who provides the answers. To be still and listen goes against our nature of wanting to be in charge.

When you find yourself in that mindset, I find the counsel of the late Dallas Willard to be very helpful: "It is much more important to cultivate the quiet, inward space of a constant listening than to always be approaching God for specific directions."[1]

Being still and listening in our times of loneliness and valley dwellings is difficult to do. It can be a long journey as you are formed, reformed, and transformed. Your spiritual transformation is an ongoing process that benefits greatly from placing yourself in the quiet presence of God and listening to his loving voice and words to you.

Knowing that our Lord is speaking to you, caring for you, and nourishing you every moment—even during all of life's valleys—makes it possible for you to proclaim every moment with full confidence: "This *is* the day that the LORD has made; let us rejoice and be glad in it."

The Seasons of Life

The steadfast love of the LORD never ceases, his mercies never come to an end;
they are new every morning ...
(Lam. 3:22-23)

I have many books on my shelf. One of them that I have enjoyed over the years is *Growing Strong in the Seasons of Life* by Charles Swindoll. Written in 1983, it includes a large variety of topics that many of us may face during our lives. I love the word "Seasons" that is included as a part of the title. That noun allows for the possibility of many different situations that have a way of appearing during our "daily walks." Some of those seasons can be times of joy and happiness while other experiences may be times of sorrow and disappointment. Perhaps the season is a time of reflection, meditation, or discernment. The opportunities and challenges that presented themselves 40 years ago in Swindoll's book still hold true today even if the details may be different. As we experience our different seasons in life, one truth remains: God is present in all of them.

You may be in a season that you thought you would never experience. It might be unemployment, a broken relationship, a pandemic, a medical situation, or some other crisis. You ask yourself, "When will it ever end?" These can be times of darkness and isolation. The days can be difficult. Often it is in times such as these that we are made stronger in our faith. Keep in mind that the journey of growing strong can be, and often is, painful. Just ask those individuals who go to the gym four days a week in an effort to "get in shape!"

On the other hand, your season of life might be a time of celebration, restoration, or spiritual renewal. You have been given the opportunity to give thanks to the Lord for his wonderful blessings to you.

Whatever season of life you might be experiencing, you can be certain of God's faithfulness. As you face a variety of seasonal challenges and blessings in your life, you can be assured that the Lord is with you in the midst of everything. God will provide all that you need. As Oswald Chambers wrote, "God does not give us overcoming life; He gives us life as we overcome."[2]

As you go through your season of life, do so with the confidence and assuredness that God will sustain and provide for you in every way. The Lord will never let you down. May you sing with the psalmist:

> And so through all the length of days
> Thy goodness faileth never;
> Good Shepherd, may I sing Thy praise
> Within Thy house forever![3]

Counting the Days

So teach us to count our days that we may gain a wise heart.
(Ps. 90:12)

Psalm 90 is one of my favorites in Scripture. I remember it best from the "old" King James Version where it begins with these words: "Lord, thou hast been our dwelling place in all generations. Before the mountains were brought forth, or even thou hadst formed the earth and the world, even from everlasting to everlasting, thou art God."

God has been God forever. There has never been a time when God wasn't around: "From everlasting to everlasting, thou art God." The whole topic of time is not an issue with God.

Later in the psalm, however, the writer instructs us to be mindful of time. My favorite verse in this psalm is where the King James Version states, "So teach us to number our days that we may apply our hearts unto wisdom" (v. 12). The psalmist is very specific in his instructions to us. We are told to number our days. While God does not operate in time, we do.

Some time ago a friend, who participated with me in a weekly Bible study, was tragically killed in a car accident not too far from our church. To us who were left behind, his days were prematurely shortened. He left this world sooner than any of us would have anticipated. Like my friend's time on earth, all of our days are numbered. As we live each day, we are asked by God to number our days so that we may apply our hearts unto wisdom. My Bible study partner did just that. He loved Jesus. That was obvious in our times together as we studied God's Word.

Our Heavenly Father wants us to use our days to commit our hearts to being filled with his wisdom. Proverbs 4:5 tells us to "Get wisdom; get insight." St. Paul reminds young Timothy in 2 Timothy 3:15, "and how from childhood you have known the sacred writings that are able to instruct you for salvation through faith in Christ Jesus."

Each day is an opportunity for us to draw nearer to the Lord and deepen our relationship with him. Number and apply are very specific instructions! Each day is a gift. God loves you and wants you to fully experience his blessings and love on a daily basis. Do not let a day go by without thanking the Lord for his gifts of another day and the opportunity to experience his love in ways that are uniquely yours. May you treasure the days the Lord provides. May you live every day for his purpose and to his glory. God bless and keep you.

Knowing the Way

I am the way and the truth and the life.
(John 14:6)

When I was a boy, my parents planned car trips to visit my grandparents. I remember watching my dad sitting at the kitchen table with maps spread out before him and studying the best possible route from Southern California to South Dakota. There was no GPS. Very few of the interstates had been completed. Two-lane roads were not uncommon. I recall that there were even some stretches of gravel roads we had to travel to reach our goal. It was important to know the way to our destination prior to starting our trip.

Knowing the way to our destination is still as important today as it was 65 years ago. Whether you are driving across town to the local outlet mall or taking a cross-country flight, you still need to know your goal and how to get there. Not knowing where you are going will ultimately lead to being lost.

It is a tragedy how many people in today's world have no idea of where they are going spiritually. They may have some generic thoughts about the hereafter and their eternal fate. However, when asked what that looks like or how one goes about getting there, they are at a loss in expressing a clear understanding of what needs to occur. They may think they know the way. They may believe that "all roads lead to the same place." But in the end, these people live a life of uncertainty. It is almost as though they get in a car and start driving without knowing their destination.

As believers in Jesus Christ go through their journey in this life, they do not need to have any uncertainty or doubts about where they are going or how to get there. They have the promise and assurance of the Lord. The resurrection of Jesus guarantees us that he is the way, the truth, and the life. Jesus is the answer to the question everyone will ask at one time or another in their life.

Jesus has traveled the road for us. He has paid all of the "tolls" along the way. Our Lord does not charge us a fare to go with him; he simply asks us to trust that he has planned the journey and will take us to our destination in this world and the next.

Our daily walks in this world can be challenging or even disappointing at times. However, we can be certain that our Lord will take us through the bumps and potholes that can come our way. Jesus knows the way because he *is* the way. Rest in that truth and place your trust in him.

Faith Walking

... for we walk by faith, not by sight.
(2 Cor. 5:7)

Not one of us can predict the future. No one knows for certain what the next 30 minutes, let alone the next 30 days, may hold for us in life's journey. We dream, we plan, we propose, and we hope. In the end, however, we cannot accurately nor with any certainty say what will happen in the future.

Most of the details yet to come in this life are a mystery. That is a reality! The good news, though, is that we do not need to know all of the details. As God's children, we know who controls the future. When our "daily walk" is grounded in a faith that trusts in our holy God—Father, Son, and Holy Spirit—who has been revealed as our provider in all things, we can move confidently, step by step through all of life's conditions.

Hebrews 11:8 is one of my favorite passages. I identify closely with it. In referring to Abraham, the author writes, "he set out, not knowing where he was going." This verse goes hand in hand with the theme verse for this devotion. Walking by faith without having all of the answers and without seeing all of the results ahead of time is something that each of us can do with confidence. We are able to do this because God has shown that we can trust him. He has a "track record."

Time and time again throughout Scripture, God came to the rescue of his children. This was demonstrated repeatedly in the Old Testament: Enoch, Noah, Abraham, Joseph, and Moses are a few examples of individuals who were guarded and blessed by God. The same can be said for Mary, Joseph, Elizabeth, Paul, Peter, and John in the New Testament. They all walked by faith, even when they could not foresee all the details of the future.

As you walk by faith, you are blessed and reassured when you remember that your Lord holds your future. There is no need to fear or doubt: God is faithful. Your future is secure not only for the next 30 minutes or 30 days, but for all of eternity.

May the Lord empower you to follow his voice even if you don't have all of the details of his plan for you. God's ways are always the best ways. Walk by faith with God.

Following the Truth

Teach me your way, O LORD, that I may walk in your truth ...
(Ps. 86:11)

Scripture relates that there were many people who were followers of Jesus at one time or another during his three-year ministry on Earth. The reasons these individuals followed our Lord were, no doubt, varied. Some may have been invited by a friend to come and hear the "new prophet" from Nazareth. Others may have heard about some of the miracles he had performed. Perhaps those individuals needed a miracle in their lives. No doubt, some people may have responded to a personal invitation Jesus offered when he spoke the words, "Follow me."

Regardless of how anyone became a follower of Jesus, we can be certain of one thing: Jesus always shared a message that was unlike any other message that had been heard. His words were always ones of truth. As Jesus' disciples and followers were listening, they were, at the same time, being equipped and empowered to live in the truth of God's message—a message that never changes, a message of hope and salvation. As people heard the Master's words, they were being given a message that would equip them not only for this life but also for eternity.

How are you able to be empowered to follow God's truth? This happens when you hear and heed the voice of the One who gives us his eternal Word. You learn God's ways for your daily walk by listening, reading, studying, and meditating upon his Word. The Lord's Spirit gives you the power and ability to follow Jesus when you "hear" God's Word.

Following the "truth" consistently only occurs when you are strengthened and filled with the power of God's Spirit. You cannot follow the "truth" in your own power. When you pray "Teach me your way, O Lord," you open yourself to the Lord and are inviting God to lead you in your daily walk so that you might be everything in this life that God wants you to be.

Jesus prayed that his disciples might be sanctified in the truth (John 17:17). The Holy Spirit prays for you (Rom. 8:26). Our Heavenly Father's will for you is to follow in his way. Studying God's Word and opening your heart to the Spirit of God provides the means for the Lord's eternal truth to guide and direct you in your daily walk.

You have a God who loves you beyond anything you can imagine. His desire for you is to walk with him and spend eternity with him. May you receive all that he has to share with you. May you walk in his truth.

Walking in God's Call

... walk in a manner worthy of the calling to which you have been called.
(Eph. 4:1)

Martin Luther suggested that an appropriate way to begin each day is by making the sign of the cross along with speaking the words of the invocation, "In the name of the Father, and of the Son, and of the Holy Spirit." Some individuals enhance this practice by applying some water to their face as a remembrance of their baptism. I include the words of St. Paul from Ephesians 4:1, "... walk in a manner worthy of the calling to which you have been called." For me, it is a good reminder that the Lord has given me a specific calling and I should be intentional in my desire to live each day and walk each day in a way that helps me fulfill that calling.

Each one of us has received a call from God. Our calls are not identical: they are specific and unique to us. The calls can range from parenthood, to singleness, to a full-time teaching or preaching ministry, to the practice of medicine, to hundreds of other possibilities. Regardless of your call, you can be assured that God had you in mind when he selected a specific purpose for your life.

But a challenge may arise when we don't listen to God's call or keep our eyes fixed on what he would have us pursue. We fail to "walk in a manner worthy" of God's call. Perhaps we become distracted, bored, discouraged, rebellious, or disinterested. We walk in other pathways from where God has called us to walk.

I'm always amazed when I watch people walk by my home. There are some who are focused on their walk, keeping their heads up and watching where they are going. They have a goal and a purpose for their walk.

Then there are others who do the complete opposite. They are walking with their phones. They are either talking to someone as they are walking or they have their heads down and are texting, not paying attention to where they are going.

It is hard to attain the goal of our calling if we are not walking in a manner that is worthy of that calling.

How do we "walk in a manner ..."? How do we "lead a life worthy ..."? By being faithful to our Lord through prayer, in hearing and studying God's Word, by receiving our Lord's gifts of grace and healing through his sacraments and ordinances, and by being open and vulnerable to the leading and guiding of the Holy Spirit.

God's call for you has divine blessing written all over it. The Lord does not make mistakes: "I have called you by name; you are mine" (Isa. 43:1). Live each day with the confidence that God *has* called you and will open doors for you to pass through. Walk in a manner worthy of God's calling, and may God bless you on your walk.

Praying When No One Is Watching

... he went up the mountain by himself to pray.
(Matt. 14:23)

One of the most precious memories I have is that of sharing a room with my grandfather for a couple of years prior to his passing. My grandmother had died unexpectedly in South Dakota in 1966. At my parents' urging, Grandpa came to live with us. I was in my first couple of years of commuting to college and also working two part-time jobs. Sharing my room was not a burden since I was away quite a bit during the daytime.

Our paths did occasionally cross, usually in the early morning and then again in the late evening prior to turning in. I recall that on a number of occasions I would come into the bedroom and see Grandpa sitting on the edge of his bed with his Bible and little prayer book. His prayer time was a regular part of his daily life. He never missed it. Seeing him pray made an impression that has stayed with me to this day.

I remember, too, my father sitting at the kitchen table praying quietly prior to eating his breakfast and leaving for work early in the dark morning hours. He did not realize that on several occasions I had gotten up early and walked quietly into the kitchen and observed him praying. His eyes were closed, his head bowed, and his hands folded. Remembering my dad like that reminds me of the words of Oswald Chambers: "My worth to God in public is what I am in private."[4]

My purpose in sharing these two stories is to encourage you to consider your prayer life and how it affects both you and others.

In his book, *With Open Hands*, Henri Nouwen reminds us: "Praying is no easy matter. It demands a relationship in which you allow someone other than yourself to enter into the very center of your being to see there what you would rather leave in darkness, and to touch there what you would rather leave untouched."[5] Brother Lawrence, a 17th-century French monk who worked in the monastery kitchen, found no difference between the daily appointed times of prayer and normal times for work. For him, prayer was the realization of always being in the presence of God.

It is easy to slip into a mindset of looking upon prayer as a type of "insurance policy" that we draw upon when the battle gets rough and the waves are overwhelming. Perhaps prayer becomes the last resort. Rather than waiting for difficult times, I would encourage you to be in prayer before, during, and after the challenges you face.

Your personal journey of being formed, reformed, and transformed will have different turns in your life. The development of your prayer life may be one of those turns. As you think about and experience the challenges you have on your daily walk, you can be inspired by those individuals who have gone before you and lived a life of prayer. St. Paul, St. Augustine, and Martin Luther are some examples who come to mind. For me, I think of my grandfather who prayed faithfully every night with his Bible and prayer book at his side, and I think of my dad who prayed even when no one was watching. God bless you and your prayer life ... especially when no one is watching.

Taking Care of God's Gifts

Like good stewards of the manifold grace of God,
serve one another with whatever gift each of you has received.
(1 Pet. 4:10)

God has given each of us a variety of gifts to manage and use for our benefit and for the good of others. In "church circles" this is commonly referred to as stewardship and relates to the "Three T's"—Time, Treasure, and Talents. The word "stewardship" is used a great deal when churches start planning a budget for the upcoming year. However, I would like to focus our thoughts toward the spiritual transformation that can occur in us when we become conscientious caretakers of what God has given to us.

All that we have is a gift from God. Martin Luther said it well in his explanation to the First Article of the Apostles' Creed: "I believe that God has made me and all creatures; that He has given me my body and soul, eyes, ears, and all my members, my reason and all my senses and still preserves them. He also gives me clothing and shoes, food and drink, house and home, wife and children, land, animals, and all I have. He richly and daily provides me with all that I need to support this body and life."[6] God owns it all, and God gives it all. The question is: "What do we do with it?"

I heard a sermon a number of years ago where it was stated that we are able to determine the priorities of an individual by looking at two books: their checkbook and their Day-Timer.® In today's day and age, checkbooks and Day-Timers are somewhat dated given the current technology. However, the thought behind the example still holds true. God gives us blessings of time, treasure, and talent every day. To what extent are we led and motivated to return God's blessings back to God and to others?

The way that we use God's gifts is an indication both of our understanding of God's care for us and our own spiritual growth and transformation. We have a God whom we can trust. God will never let us down and will always provide for us just what we need, and exactly when we need it. Let the words of the hymn writer be our prayer:

> Take my life and let it be
> Consecrated Lord to Thee;
> Take my moments and my days,
> Let them flow in ceaseless praise.
>
> Take my love, my Lord I pour
> At Thy feet its treasure store;
> Take myself and I will be
> Ever, only, all for Thee.[7]

May you be encouraged to remember and experience the many blessings God continues to share each day. God bless you on your journey of caring for God's gifts to you.

Always Keep on Singing

About midnight Paul and Silas were praying and singing hymns ...
(Acts 16:25)

I wonder how many of us would be singing at midnight if we were locked up and chained in jail. Perhaps we would be praying, but I suspect that singing would be a distant thought for most of us. For Paul and Silas, though, it was as natural as putting one foot in front of the other to walk.

Music is one of God's great gifts to us. Can you imagine a world without music? It would be like living in a world without the vibrant colors God has placed in Creation. Singing is one expression of that gift. It is a way in which we can respond to God's blessings and also express our faith, our emotions, and our needs as we take our "daily walks" on life's journey. Worship Pastor Glenn Packiam writes: "Christians don't sing simply because we're happy; we sing because we are people of hope."[8]

Think about that statement. Not all of life's situations are "happy" times. Yet even in the times of sadness and despair and the challenges we all face, Christians are still able to be people of hope. We sing at memorial services and funerals. We sing during times of personal disappointments. We raise our voices and sing as a nation during uncertain times of war and natural disasters. The book of Psalms implores us again and again to "Sing to the Lord" and "Make a joyful noise to the Lord." As God's "Easter people," we can do that with confidence. When we sing, we draw near to the Lord. As the phrase often attributed to St. Augustine states, "They who sing pray twice."

During my years as a choral director, I only had a couple of "rules" with my choirs. One of them was "Always keep on singing." We sing because we are people of hope. Our hope is in the cross and resurrection of Jesus. That is always worth singing about.

"Always keep on singing."

Recognizing God's Vision

I was not disobedient to the heavenly vision ...
(Acts 26:19)

Acts 26 relates St. Paul's strong defense before King Agrippa. As part of that defense, Paul testifies to his unwavering faith: "I was not disobedient to the heavenly vision" (v. 19). Paul is referring to his conversion experience on the road to Damascus described in Acts 9:1-9. It was at his conversion moment when he realized that his life would never be the same. Over the course of time, God's plan, God's vision for Paul, was revealed. It changed Paul's life. He testified of his own faithfulness to that vision. To recognize God's vision for himself, Paul had to be knocked off of his horse and blinded for three days. Isn't it ironic? For Paul to "see" God's vision, he had to be without sight for a period of time.

How are you doing in seeing God's vision for your life? Where is your sight focused? Are you using God's gift to more clearly discern his plan for your life? Jeremiah 29:11 speaks of God's plan for you. What actions are you taking to help you in recognizing those plans? I would like to make three suggestions that may be helpful as you seek to become more aware of God's unique vision for you.

First, keep your eyes on Jesus. One of my favorite passages is Hebrews 12:1-2 where the writer says, "... let us run with perseverance the race that is set before us, looking to Jesus, the pioneer and perfecter of our faith ..." There are many distractions in this world that seek to get us to focus on something other than Jesus. The things of this life, both good and bad, are never a substitute for what Jesus brings to us.

Second, use your ears: listen to God's still, small voice. I love the story in 1 Kings 19 where Elijah is fleeing from Jezebel. He is standing on a mountain, waiting for a word from the Lord. God does not speak in the wind, or the earthquake, or the fire. No, God speaks in the "gentle blowing." For Elijah to hear God's voice in the "gentle blowing," he needed to be listening.

Third, when God reveals his vision for you—whatever it may be—do not hesitate to embark on that journey. Remove yourself from any circumstances that may prevent you from responding to God's call. When Jesus calls you to action, do not hesitate to respond. Rather, speak the words, "Here I am, Lord."

Keep your eyes on Jesus. Listen for God's voice. Respond when the vision and call are before you. God *does* have plans for each of us. May you always be in tune to God so that you might obey him and receive his blessing upon your life. God bless you.

The "Eyes" Have It

To you I lift up my eyes ...
(Ps. 123:1)

During the years of my ministry, I have attended many congregational meetings—too many to count. Many of them included spiritual topics, reports, and church business. One thing that was usually part of these meetings was the opportunity to vote on resolutions, accepting the minutes "as reported," or voting to call a pastor or other ministry leader. It was not uncommon for the person chairing the meeting to speak the words, "The ayes (pronounced I's) have it," following the vote.

That phrase caused me to think about our "EYES." As Shakespeare said, "The eyes are the window to the soul." Scripture mentions eyes in a number of different contexts.

In Proverbs 23:26 Solomon instructs us to "let your *eyes* observe [God's] ways." Paul writes in Ephesians 1:18 "so that, with the *eyes* of your heart enlightened you may know what is the hope to which he has called you ..." In Psalm 121:1 the psalmist says, "I lift up my *eyes* to the hills ..." And in Psalm 123:1-2 the writer states: "To you I lift up my *eyes*, O you who are enthroned in the heavens! As the *eyes* of servants look to the hand of their master, as the *eyes* of a maid to the hand of her mistress, so our *eyes* look to the LORD our God, until he has mercy upon us."

Our eyes are very important not only for our day-to-day existence, but also, and more importantly, for focusing upon the things of God. Whether we are running a spiritual race, seeking enlightenment, looking to the Lord for direction and help, or waiting upon the Lord for his gracious action in our life, we need to keep our eyes focused on him.

How do you use your eyes? Are they focused on the things of God? Are your eyes the window to your soul? It has been said that a sure way of learning more about a person is simply by looking into their eyes.

If our eyes are focused on Jesus, we can be sure that our message to the world will be one of love, concern, and compassion. We will be certain the "*eyes*" really do have it! May God keep all of you as you keep your eyes on him.

The Gift of "Do-Overs"

I will put enmity between you and the woman ...
(Gen. 3:15)

I am not a huge tennis fan. I do, however, enjoy watching the major tournaments. The French Open, Wimbledon, and the U.S. Open are "Must See TV." As we move into the spring and then later into summer, I enjoy watching Rafael Nadal and the other great players display their skills in those highly competitive events.

To the best of my knowledge, tennis is the only sport that allows for "do-overs." The USGA (golf) doesn't allow "mulligan" shots. The NFL (football) doesn't give the kicker a second opportunity if he misses a field goal. MLB (baseball) doesn't allow "strike four." Yet in tennis, the players are given a second chance, a do-over, if they miss-hit their first serve or if the ball touches the net on the first serve. They get an additional opportunity to erase the first misplay.

Our lives as Christians are similar to that aspect of the game of tennis. Because of what Jesus has done for us, we are given a second chance. God is in the "second chance" business. Think about it: Adam and Eve received a second chance after the Fall (Gen. 3:15). The children of Israel received numerous do-overs throughout the Old Testament. King David was given a second chance after his sin with Bathsheba and against Uriah (2 Sam. 12:13). Peter was forgiven by Jesus after he denied his Savior three times (John 21:15-17).

Do-overs and second chances don't necessarily negate the consequences of the first mistake. If Rafael Nadal misplays his first serve, he will need to be less aggressive on his second serve. That gives his opponent a better opportunity to return the serve and win the point. Adam and Eve were expelled from the Garden of Eden. King David's infant son died seven days after his birth. While do-overs may not erase the pain of the initial mistake, God's second chances assure us that he continually loves us and promises to be with us, sustain us, and guard us as we live in the hope of eternal life and resurrection.

All of us have miss-hit many first serves in our life. Because we have the condition of original sin within us, we will always be challenged. But thanks be to God for his gift of salvation for each of us.

Jesus came, died, and rose from the dead to give us a second chance. May all of us continue to live with the reality of Easter hope and joy. Because Jesus lives, our future is secure. Christ is risen. He is risen indeed. Alleluia!

Temptations: We All Have Them

For we do not have a high priest who is unable to sympathize with our weaknesses ...
(Heb. 4:15)

I don't know about you, but when I see a slice of devil's food cake with chocolate frosting, I'm tempted to dive right in and enjoy it. The only thing that might slow me down is taking the time to place a large scoop of vanilla ice cream alongside the cake!

Temptations: we all have them. They come in all shapes, sizes, and descriptions. Some temptations are harmless, but others can lead to harmful results.

During the season of Lent, that 40-day period (not counting Sundays) when we are mindful of the passion of Jesus, the biblical story of Jesus' 40-day stay in the wilderness can help us focus on our own temptations. After fasting for 40 days, Jesus was tempted by Satan three different times. Each time, though, Jesus rebuffed the temptation with the Word of God.

Jesus' time in the wilderness was not the only time he was tempted. Hebrews 4:15 tells us, "For we do not have a high priest who is unable to sympathize with our weaknesses, but we have one who in every respect has been tested as we are, yet without sin." Jesus still understands what it is like to be tempted: he experienced temptation firsthand, yet he didn't sin. He was victorious over sin, death, and the devil.

In the sixth petition of The Lord's Prayer we pray, "and lead us not into temptation." Martin Luther explained that "God tempts no one."[9] We are encouraged by Luther that when we are tempted, we should pray "that God would guard and keep us so that the devil, the world, and our sinful nature may not deceive us or mislead us into false belief, despair, and other great shame and vice."[10]

Each day we have one opportunity after another to draw closer to the Lord and feel his protective arms around us. We will continue to be tempted by a variety of things in life. As the accounts of Jesus' temptations in Matthew and Luke relate, we can fight those temptations that Satan puts before us with the Word of God. In those times when we fail, we can be certain that when we repent, God will be there to place arms of love and forgiveness around us.

Jesus went through his 40 days in the wilderness and traveled "the way of the Cross" so that when we fall, we will not find ourselves in a hopeless situation. Rather, we will see a loving Savior who has faced the same temptations we have, ready to receive us.

May your daily journey always include a time of reflection upon what Jesus has done for you. God bless you.

Obeying God's Voice

The word of the LORD came to Jonah a second time ...
(Jonah 3:1)

Each of us hears a variety of voices in our lifetime. Our "daily walks" pass through many different conversations, explanations, instructions, and "words of wisdom." The din of verbal noise is always present in our world unless we intentionally look for those times and places when we can experience peace and quiet.

It is during those times when we are able to be selective in what we listen for that we often hear God's voice. Being aware of the reality that the Lord may have a message for us is an important part of life's journey. When we hear the Lord's word for us, it is important to respond to what is being spoken. Failure to obey can, and often does, lead to circumstances and conditions that place us in a situation of sorrow, despair, or disappointment.

The prophet Jonah was given a specific message from God but failed to respond in the way the Lord requested. Not only did Jonah ignore the message, but he also chose to make a decision that was completely opposite of what the Lord instructed. On some occasions we hear the saying, "Ignorance of the law is no excuse." Jonah had no excuse. He knew exactly what God wanted, yet he still chose to ignore the message. Jonah's response led to being in the belly of a large fish for three days and nights, a situation that none of us would want to experience. But then, "The word of the LORD came to Jonah a second time." God gave Jonah a second opportunity to respond favorably to the Lord's original message. Think for a moment how much sorrow and discomfort Jonah would have avoided if he had obeyed God the first time.

Perhaps we need to ask ourselves the question, "How much pain and disappointment could I avoid if I obey God's voice when he first speaks to me?" How many times have you had an excuse or ignored God's voice, and, as a result, experienced a condition you would rather have avoided?

Obeying the words of the world may, or may not, lead to a positive or negative result, depending upon what those words are conveying. On the other hand, listening to God's words and following God's will always leads to peace and a unique plan for each of us.

It took Jonah two times before he got "it" right. We have the advantage of learning from Jonah's experience and receiving God's best for us the first time.

May your ears be open, your heart receptive, and your voice responding with the words, "Lord, I am listening. I hear you. I am ready to obey." May God bless you as you obey his word for you.

Where Are Your Thoughts?

Set your minds on the things that are above, not on the things that are on earth ...
(Col. 3:2)

We live in a fallen world. Much of what we see and experience in our daily walk is not what God intended for us. Because we exist in some conditions and situations that are far different than God's original plan, we are faced with choices that require us to focus upon who we are and whose we are.

As God's children, we have the opportunity and privilege to live a life that operates on a completely different plane than the world. Because we belong to the Lord, we have been given the presence and power of the Holy Spirit to guide and direct us in our decisions and daily living. We can lead Spirit-directed lives that demonstrate God's redemptive presence. Despite this reality, we still struggle with decisions, thoughts, and temptations because we have a sinful nature that is constantly trying to lead us astray.

Acknowledging that fact and confessing our areas of weakness and sin to God and then receiving forgiveness is a wonderful start to being able to follow St. Paul's exhortation to "set your minds on the things that are above ..." Paul's words do not imply that we should not deal with those areas in our earthly life that provide all of the blessings the Lord would have us experience in our day-to-day living.

We do, in fact, give attention to family and relational responsibilities. We plan our finances. We think about and prepare for those potential circumstances that may cross our paths in the weeks, months, and years that are yet to come. Our Lord encourages us to make wise decisions about those kinds of things without them becoming distractions that might encourage us to take our mind off of those areas that are of an eternal nature.

While we journey through this life and make God-pleasing decisions regarding the "here and now," St. Paul encourages us to focus our thoughts and decisions on the things of God, those things that are "above." Many times, those things that "are above" can be realized in those thoughts that relate to "the things that are on earth." A decision regarding being part of a questionable relationship or entering into a "shady" business undertaking in the present will, in fact, have consequences that relate to those "things that are above."

One phrase that has become common in the present-day Christian community is, "What would Jesus do?" Perhaps we ask that question to help us deal with situations that are "on the earth." In coming to a God-pleasing response, we can recognize that we have actually focused on the Lord's will for us and those "things that are above."

May your minds and thoughts be continually and foremost centered upon the things of God and God's perfect will for you.

Let God Love You

... the love that God has for us.
(1 John 4:16)

Some people have been blessed with individuals in their life who have influenced their thinking and understanding of Scripture and also their daily walk with the Lord. For me, one of those individuals was the late Lloyd Ogilvie, the 61st chaplain of the United States Senate who served from 1995 to 2003.

Prior to his chaplaincy, Dr. Ogilvie was pastor of the First Presbyterian Church of Hollywood, California from 1972 to 1995. It was during the 1980s that I first became acquainted with Dr. Ogilvie and his preaching through his television and radio ministry program, *Let God Love You*. Dr. Ogilvie was one of the finest preachers I have ever heard. His messages always conveyed God's love and allowed that love to permeate and influence viewers and listeners who heard his powerful words.

The phrase, "Let God love you," has caused me to reflect and ask the question, "Do I let God love me?" Do you let God love you? Do you live each moment of every day with the awareness and belief that God loves you? God's love is available to each of us every day. It's never a question of whether or not God loves us: God's love is all-encompassing. "For God so loved the world ..." (John 3:16). The question is whether we live in the reality of that love. Do you accept what God freely offers? Do you ask for God's love and power in your life? It's readily available, you know! Psalm 86:5 says, "For you, O Lord, are good and forgiving, abounding in steadfast love to all who call on you."

The Apostle John's first epistle speaks a lot about the nature of God and God's love for us. One passage that stands out is 1 John 4:16 where he writes, "So we have known and believe the love that God has for us." As Jesus said, "Come to me" (Matt. 11:28), we are reminded that God's love is available to each of us. We are reminded by the prophet in Jeremiah 29:13, "When you search for me, you will find me; if you seek me with all your heart."

The Christian life is an active one. It seeks, searches, and willingly receives all of the wonderful gifts God has to offer. This life depends upon God to take us through the many challenges we face and lead us to all of God's wonderful blessings and the gift of life with him. The Christian life desires God's love.

My prayer is that each of you will open yourselves to the great love that God offers to you through his Son, Jesus, and that you will live in the power of that love (2 Tim. 1:7). Let God love you!

The Greatest Thing

... and the greatest of these is love.
(1 Cor. 13:13)

In John Baille's classic devotional, *A Diary of Private Prayer*, written in 1936, the Scottish theologian includes this prayer for the 23rd day of the month: "Holy Father, from whom all good things come, let the Christian gifts of faith, hope, and love be more firmly established in me every day."[11]

While meditating on this prayer on several occasions, I have been reminded of St. Paul's writings from 1 Corinthians 13 where he talks about faith, hope, and love. Most of us are familiar with verse 13 in that chapter: "And now faith, hope, and love remain, these three, and the greatest of these is love."

Faith is a key ingredient in our Christian walk. It is one of Martin Luther's three great *solas*. Some theologians suggest that the word "trust" is an even stronger word than "faith." Trust infers total commitment. It's like the small child who takes the hand of her parents in a busy mall or when crossing the street. The child has no doubt that she will be safe as long as she holds on and trusts.

Secondly, there is the component of *hope*. We often hear this word used as expressing a desire. "I *hope* that everything works out." "I *hope* that my team wins." In a theological sense, however, we think in terms such as "My *hope* is built on nothing less than Jesus' blood and righteousness."[12] When we use hope in that sense, we are saying, "I have no doubt that God will care for me now and in the future." We can also consider this definition: "Hope is the opposite of despair." Despair implies having no future. Hope in Jesus is the complete opposite. We know that we have a future because we know who holds the future.

Despite the wonderful benefits we receive from faith and hope, Paul finishes by saying that the greatest quality is love. What is it that distinguishes love from faith and hope?

Love never fails. In our walk, we may have occasional doubts, fears, and setbacks. But love *never* fails. Why? Because "God is love" (1 John 4:8). God's love is perfect. It never fails! St. John implores us to "love one another, because love is from God; everyone who loves is born of God and knows God" (1 John 4:7). The qualities of love reflect patience and kindness. In love there is no jealousy or arrogance (1 Cor. 13:4-6). When we walk as a child of the Light (1 John 1:5-7) we reflect God's love, a perfect love, for the world to see.

Keep the faith. Don't lose hope. Most importantly, practice love in all that you do.

Unexpected Suprises

When it was evening on that day ...
Jesus came and stood among them and said, "Peace be with you."
(John 20:19)

I have never been a big fan of surprises. There are, of course, some occasions that are referred to as "pleasant surprises." Those times can be enjoyable. However, my own experiences, for the most part, have led me to try and avoid surprises if possible.

When I was directing church choirs on a full-time basis, I asked the choir members to "Let me know when you know." In other words, if it was necessary for a member to miss a rehearsal, let me know when you first know. Don't wait until the last minute and "surprise" me. I didn't want to walk into a 7:30 p.m. rehearsal at 7:29 and find out that three of my four tenors would not be present!

Jesus, on the other hand, loved surprises! He was always ready to reveal something about himself that came as a complete surprise to his disciples and those around him. Think about it: On one occasion he was dealing with 5,000 men plus women and children who were hungry and tired. What did he do with five loaves and two fish? He surprised the crowd and fed them. Another time, Jesus took seven loaves of bread and fed more than 4,000 people. Surprise! Surprise!

There was the time when Jesus was asleep in the boat during a big storm. The disciples were panicking. Full of fear, they awakened Jesus. What did he do? He surprised them by stilling the storm. On another occasion, Jesus surprised Mary, Martha, and the disciples with the words, "Lazarus, come forth!" What happened? Lazarus came forth. Lazarus had been dead for four days. Surprise! Surprise!

It was the Sunday morning following the death of Jesus on Good Friday. The women were on their way to tend to Jesus' body. Big surprise: Jesus wasn't there; he had risen from the dead. That night, the disciples were secluded in a room hiding from the Jews. What happened? Jesus appeared and said, "Peace be with you." That's the last thing the disciples were expecting. Surprise! Surprise!

I will never forget the words of my district bishop when he learned that I would be moving from Southern California to Virginia to serve in another congregation. He said, "Wally, our God is a God of surprises!"

One thing that I have learned through the years is that while the "surprises" we share with one another may not always be appreciated or beneficial, the surprises that God shares with us usually come when we least expect them and when we need them the most.

God's blessings to us should never come as a surprise. Time and time again, God demonstrates his love and mercy to us in myriads of ways. God has been faithful in the past, is faithful now, and will continue to be faithful. God loves us and provides for us. God is always with us. That should come as no surprise!

Never Far Away

... I am with you always ...
(Matt. 28:20)

Do you remember the final words Jesus spoke to his disciples prior to his ascension into heaven? "And remember, I am with you always, to the end of the age" (Matt. 28:20). I was reminded of that scripture passage one morning during a time of personal devotion.

One of the prayers from John Baille's *A Diary of Private Prayer* includes this petition: "O God, give me today a strong and vivid sense that you are by my side. In a crowd or by myself, in business and leisure, in my sitting down and my rising, may I always be aware of your presence beside me."[13]

Our wonderful God has promised to be with us in all of our circumstances. He never forsakes us or leaves us. The Lord is near in whatever situation we might be facing. Whether we are on a mountain peak or in a dark valley, God is there with us.

Selected verses from Psalm 139 come to mind as we think about the reality of God's presence in our lives: "Where can I go from your spirit? Or where can I flee from your presence? If I ascend to heaven, you are there; if I make my bed in Sheol, you are there. If I take the wings of the morning, and settle at the farthest limits of the sea, even there your hand shall lead me, and your right hand shall hold me fast" (vv. 7-10).

The Lord is always with his children—that's us! No problem is too large, no disappointment so severe, no broken relationship or hurtful word so great, no situation in life so puzzling that our Lord will not come alongside us to lift us up, restore us, and carry us.

Can you imagine the questions the disciples must have had as they saw Jesus ascend? Perhaps some of us have the same questions. As we live with all of the challenges and questions of the 21st century and these uncertain times, remember the words of Jesus: "I am with you always." He will never fail us or forsake us.

Christ has died! Christ is risen! Christ will come again! God's peace to you.

Wide Seas, Small Boats

A windstorm suddenly arose on the sea,
so great that the boat was being swamped by the waves ...
(Matt. 8:24)

When I read the story of Jesus stilling the storm, found in Matthew 8:23-27, I am reminded of the old Breton Fisherman's Prayer. "Dear God, be good to me. The sea is so wide and my boat is so small."

Jesus was asleep. The wind was raging. Water was filling the boat. The disciples were scared to death. "Lord, save us! We are perishing!" (Matt. 8:25). While the disciples' reaction to the storm was one of fear, Jesus' response was quite the opposite. "'Why are you afraid, you of little faith?' Then he got up and rebuked the winds and the sea, and there was a dead calm" (Matt. 8:26-27).

For Jesus, it was business as usual. There was a raging sea and howling winds, and, at best, a modest-size fishing boat filled to capacity, ill-equipped to survive the tempest. The conditions created a situation that tested each disciple's faith to its limit. While it is doubtful that the disciples were wearing life jackets, they had someone with them that was a far greater lifesaver than a life jacket: Jesus was with them the entire time.

The same holds true for each of us. Often, we face similar conditions in our daily walk. We find ourselves confronted by conditions and problems that overwhelm us. We are attempting to do our best in coping with everything before us, literally trying to "keep our head above water." Then, suddenly, we find ourselves surrounded by rough seas and in a boat that we believe is too small to face the stormy waters that life places before us.

Our Lord Jesus, the one who has overcome every storm in life through his death and resurrection, is always with us, in our boat regardless of the the size. Even when it seems as though we cannot navigate through life's storms in our small boat, we can be confident that Jesus will be with us at our side to guide us and guard us through the deep waters. Trust the captain of your salvation (Heb. 2:10 KJV) and place your faith in him. He promises to always guide and guard you.

Your sea may be wide and your boat may seem small, but Jesus is with you. He calms the storms in your life and gives you his peace.

Winners and Losers

And this is the victory that conquers the world, our faith.
(1 John 5:4)

I have a little paperback book on my shelf titled *Winners and Losers*. Given to me about 50 years ago, it is comprised of brief sayings that compare "winners and losers." One sampling is "A winner makes commitments; a loser makes promises."[14] Another example of the content is "A winner says, 'Let's find out,' a loser says, 'Nobody knows.'"[15] As you can see, this book is not a "theological giant!" However, I have kept it over the years simply because I occasionally like to find a reference that makes a good comparison between different perspectives or ideas.

Some of us may have categorized someone or something as a winner or loser at one time or another. It's easy to let those words carelessly roll past our lips without giving much thought to the unkind message they may convey. Referring to someone as a "loser" does not define a spirit of Christian charity or kindness. There are other ways to express disapproval or disappointment with certain actions or behavior that may cross our path.

Having said that, there are appropriate times when we can refer to those individuals or groups of people who are either victorious or who, on the other hand, fail to achieve victory. We watch athletic contests with an expectation that one team will win and the other will lose. Political elections have winners and losers.

The journey we have on Earth affords us the opportunity to be eternally victorious. Our victory, though, is not because of anything we do. As Christians, we have been given the gift of faith by the Holy Spirit to receive the victory that Jesus won for us when he died on the cross, rose from the dead three days later, and defeated the devil. Jesus' victory over death did not require extra innings or an overtime period. His victory assures us that those who by faith receive his gift are truly "winners."

There are some who choose not to receive the results of Jesus' victory. There is still time for us to do our part to share the wonderful story of the Lord's conquering sin, death, and the devil with those people. God wants everyone to be "winners." God doesn't look upon unbelievers as "losers." Rather, God looks upon them as he looks upon all of his children who needed a Savior and those who still need a Savior. God has provided the "Way" for all to become "winners."

I pray that each of us who know the Lord will do our part to share the wonderful gospel story with those who still need to receive it. May sharing the message of hope and salvation be a part of your daily walk on your journey.

Living in the Clouds

Your steadfast love, O LORD, extends to the heavens, your faithfulness to the clouds.
(Ps. 36:5)

Someone who is described as having their "head in the clouds" is not usually thought of as one who can be relied upon. They likely give an impression of being absentminded or impractical. You would not likely enter into an important business decision with such a person. Rather than having our head in the clouds, we are encouraged and expected to keep our "feet on the ground" if we want to be taken seriously and looked upon as one who is responsible and well-grounded.

For the most part, that is true, despite the fact that some of the greatest inventors and thinkers in history were often thought of as "dreamers."

As Christians, our feet are planted firmly on the death and resurrection of Jesus. He is the Rock of our Salvation. While we live in that assurance every day, we also face times when we need daily reminders of God's love and faithfulness. The enemy's role is clear: he wants to discourage and distract us from our journey with the Lord. When we face bumps on the road, we can be certain that Satan will do his best to tempt us to take our focus off of the Lord and doubt God's love for us.

When those times cross our path, we need to be reminded of the psalmist's words in Psalm 36:5. God's love extends to the heavens. His faithfulness rises to the clouds. In other words, we are always surrounded and encompassed by God's mercy and presence. As God's children, we are always covered. God's love and faithfulness for us is present in this world and beyond into the heavens. His mercy knows no limit. While we are limited by time and space, God cares for us beyond our own boundaries.

May you walk with your faith firmly planted in Jesus Christ, and with the knowledge that God's faithfulness and love for you surpass this present world to the heights of heaven and beyond.

The Vicissitudes of Life

Many are the afflictions of the righteous, but the LORD rescues them from them all.
(Ps. 34:19)

One of my mentors early in my ministry used to talk about "the vicissitudes of life." We served together for almost 20 years in parish ministry. I can still remember how he would simply let the word "vicissitudes" roll off the end of his tongue. He always had a slight smile on his face as he spoke it. Despite that smile, he would talk about vicissitudes from a perspective of authority and first-hand experience.

Prior to serving as our senior pastor, he had served as a Navy chaplain in Vietnam during the height of the Vietnam conflict. More than once, he spoke of the many heartaches and loss of life he had witnessed. He often shared remembrances of ministering to service men and women and their families as they experienced the "vicissitudes of life." His ministry, both in Vietnam and when I worked with him in the parish, was always a "gospel ministry," one of hope and comfort. He showed the love of Jesus and brought comfort and hope to those whom he served as they faced their challenging times.

Psalm 34:19 is a reminder that all of us will experience various vicissitudes as we go through life's journey. There is no escaping the fact that we all deal with episodes in life that we would rather avoid. Disappointments, illnesses, relationship challenges, problems at work/school/home, and times of emotional and spiritual valleys are just a few of the "afflictions" we can face as we move from day to day. That is a reality, but there is good news! Our Lord is with us through all of these challenges. He rescues us from those situations. God's rescue plan may be different than our plan would be. As a matter of fact, you can count on the certainty that God's plan is better than any we might envision. His ways are always better than our ways.

The Christian walk is a journey of faith (2 Cor. 5:7). As we walk by faith, we have God's assurance that he will always be with us before, during, and after we experience the "vicissitudes of life." God is in the "rescue business." That's why Jesus died for us. Rescuing is what the Lord does best! Thank you, Lord.

Words of Invitation

Come to me ...
(Matt. 11:28)

I don't know too many people who enjoy being ignored or "left out." Most of us want to be included. Whether it's a party, a sporting event, a nice dinner, a book study, a group activity with friends, or some other occasion, most everyone likes to feel included. Receiving a letter in the mail, getting a phone call, or opening an E-vite with a fancy RSVP—all of these invitations are affirmations that someone cares enough about you to ask you to be a part of something special.

When Jesus says, "Come to me," he is asking you to be a part of something very significant. He is offering you a better way than the world offers. He is inviting you to a new way. As you go through life's journey, you see many different paths that offer peace and happiness. Without exception, all of the world's paths are lacking in securing the peace and serenity that Jesus offers. He says, "Come to me." He offers you rest. He says that you can learn from him. He promises gifts that no one else is able to deliver. He gives the gift of eternal life. Many individuals and "programs" in this world make promises, but Jesus fulfills his promises.

If you are reading these thoughts, there is a good chance that you agree with what has been written. You have recognized and accepted the blessings that Jesus offers. Praise God for that!

But what can be said about those people who have not heard the invitation Jesus offers? Jesus speaks the same words to them: "Come to me." You have heard those words and by God's grace and mercy have responded to Jesus' invitation. Throughout your life you will interact with friends, family members, colleagues, neighbors, and strangers who have not heard these words of Jesus.

Will you be the messenger of Jesus' words to one of those individuals? Will you ask the Lord to empower you with his Holy Spirit so that you can share Jesus' invitation? There are many people who have never responded to Jesus' invitation of "Come to me" because they have never been invited. Don't leave them out. Don't ignore them. Offer them an invitation to the same "special event" that you are experiencing.

I pray that you will invite others to come to Jesus just as he has invited you. God bless you.

A New Beginning

I am about to do a new thing ...
(Isa. 43:18-19)

I started taking piano lessons when I was 6 years old. As I grew older, my mother and piano teacher "encouraged" me to "practice, practice, practice!" But practicing piano, especially at an early age, was not my favorite pastime. I would have preferred to go outside and play baseball with my friends.

When I practiced, I would often come to a difficult passage in the music, stop, and start over at the beginning. It seemed that I could not get past a certain point. Over time, however, I discovered that if I isolated and worked on the difficult passages, I would have greater success in learning and performing the music. The more I worked on the difficult part, the better it got. It was as though there was a new beginning. I no longer "remembered" how to play the music incorrectly. Rather, I played it accurately and the way the composer had intended.

Your journey through life can be a lot like trying to learn how to play an instrument or learn a piece of music. You face problems, challenges, disappointments, and other circumstances that seemingly cannot be overcome. You try to stop, to ignore, or to walk around those obstacles but are not successful. The old methodology you have used simply doesn't work.

There may be situations that require you to think differently about issues in your life that are either temporary or seemingly permanent. It may be a small issue or a life-changing decision that will require a whole new beginning. Perhaps it is a new job, getting married, or moving across the country. Maybe it is coming to grips with a spiritual condition that requires you to deny your "old" self and become the "new" person God wants you to be.

Throughout Scripture, God calls people to do away with a former way of life and to undergo a new beginning, a significant change: "Now the LORD said to Abram, 'Go from your country and your kindred and your father's house to the land that I will show you'" (Gen. 12:1)... A new beginning for Abraham. "So Moses took his wife and his sons, put them on a donkey, and went back to the land of Egypt" (Exod. 4:20)... A new beginning for Moses. "So Boaz took Ruth, and she became his wife" (Ruth 4:13)... A new beginning for Ruth. "He fell to the ground and heard a voice saying to him, 'Saul, Saul, why do you persecute me?'" (Acts 9:4)... A new beginning for St. Paul.

What "former" things might God be asking you to forget so that he can make something "new" in your life? That "new" may be as simple as correcting the wrong notes on a piano piece or as faith-stretching as setting out to a new land, not knowing where you are going (Heb. 11:8). Be aware that God may come to you with a "change" when you least expect it. His change may make no sense to you. But you can be certain that whatever you are called to do, the Lord will be honored, and you will be blessed in new and wonderful ways.

Givers of Peace

Peace I leave with you; my peace I give to you.
(John 14:27)

Jesus brings peace. Jesus is the one who shares his peace to quell every fear we experience in our lives. Throughout his earthly ministry, Jesus not only talked about peace and peacemakers (Matt. 5:9), but he also personified peace in his actions and deeds.

It should be no surprise that in some of the final moments with his disciples prior to his death, Jesus gave a personal assurance of peace: "Peace I leave with you; my peace I give to you" (John 14:27). That message must have been very important for Jesus to include it in that precious time.

The next several days must have seemed like an eternity for the Lord's friends. Jesus had been betrayed and crucified. He was dead. But then the world turned upside down. Jesus rose from the dead! He was alive! The disciples had heard the news from some of the women, but they weren't necessarily convinced. Then Jesus appeared to them on that first Easter Sunday night. The first words out of his mouth were, "Peace be with you" (John 20:21). A week later, with Thomas present, Jesus appeared again. His first words were, "Peace be with you" (John 20:26).

Jesus had three opportunities to speak any word, give any gift, or perform any miracle. What did he do? He gave the gift of peace. Jesus' gift of peace was important to his disciples, and it is important to us. As followers of Jesus, what do we do with his gift of peace? We give his peace to others.

We live in a world that is hurting and lives in pain and suffering. It is a world that experiences never-ending conflicts and war. We see relationships and families torn apart by anger and turmoil. None of us needs to look very far to see where we can share the peace of Jesus.

One of my favorite sayings that I remember from a professor is, "You need to be an agent of change." In a fallen world that cries out for peace, we all need to be agents of change. We need to be givers of Jesus' peace. World leaders and nations talk about "peace." However, it is only the peace of Jesus that can heal our wounds and bring eternal security to each of us. The peace that Jesus gives is an everlasting peace, one that places us in the arms of the Eternal God who loves us and cares for us.

Experiencing the reality of knowing God's peace removes all fear from our hearts and minds. May you take the gift of peace that Jesus offers and share it with those in your life. It is a gift that will change lives forever.

Imitating God

*Therefore be imitators of God, as beloved children,
and walk in love, as Christ loved us ...*
(Eph. 5:1-2)

Many people have heard the saying, "Imitation is the sincerest form of flattery." It has been attributed to the 19th-century Irish poet and playwright Oscar Wilde. The thought behind the saying is generally considered to be a compliment, one of admiration. One person values some attributes they see in another person and tries to emulate those qualities in their own life.

It is not uncommon for students who have been influenced by a teacher or mentor to imitate and apply many of the characteristics and qualities they have observed in an academic or professional setting. Relying upon and using positive and powerful experiences we have received from those who have taught and influenced us is a wonderful blessing that can be very beneficial.

Life's journey affords us many opportunities to learn from others and imitate their teachings and life lessons in our own situations. Using what we gain from others can help us navigate our daily walk.

While we may have respected mentors or colleagues from whom we have gleaned knowledge and choose to imitate, the greatest teacher we can look to and learn from is our loving God. He has much to teach us, and we have much that we need to learn and apply to our life. God is love (1 John 4:7). His love is perfect and never-ending. God has shown us that love in his Son, Jesus Christ. The greatest way we can be imitators of God is by sharing the love we receive through Jesus. We can do this, not by our own power, but through the power of God's Holy Spirit.

The phrase, "What would Jesus do?" has become a common saying over the past few years. In many instances, that question is referred to when someone is faced with making a decision that causes them to pause or hesitate in offering an answer. Perhaps one way of answering the question is with another question: "Would I be imitating God with what I decide to do?"

One answer, however, that you can always be certain of when asking this question is, "Imitate God and show his love by the power of the Holy Spirit." By showing God's love in every situation, you will be the imitator that God wants you to be. You will be blessing the lives of those with whom you walk.

"Beloved, since God loved us so much, we also ought to love one another" (1 John 4:11). Be an imitator!

Part 2

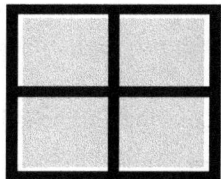

Prayers for the Daily Walk

... for the start of a new week

Gracious Lord God,

On this first day of the week, I take a moment in time and thank you for your care and provision in the days I have already lived. At the same time I look at what lies before me, both known and unknown, in the coming seven days that will reveal themselves.

There are plans that have been prepared and events and circumstances known only to you that will be unveiled to me in your time. While I would like to believe that I have control over those plans that are on my mind or on my calendar, the reality is that only you know the master plan and events that will meet me in my journey this week.

It is in recognizing this reality, Lord, that I enter this new week, trusting you for your guidance, wisdom, and protection for me and for those I hold most dear. May I walk with my eyes and mind fixed solely on you, being assured that I am in your care and love. May I be in conversation with you during every moment of the days before me.

May I experience and feel your presence, power, and love in every action, word, and thought that I may share and express in all of my circumstances in the days ahead. I trust you, Lord, to direct and guide this week. In your name, I pray. Amen.

> I am trusting Thee to guide me;
> Thou alone shalt lead,
> Ev'ry day and hour supplying
> All my need.[16]

... for the beginning of the day

Dear Lord,

I come to you in this morning hour with thanks for the gift of a peaceful evening's sleep and rest. I praise you for the beginning of a new day and an awareness of the love and mercy you have for me. May I enter this moment in time with the assurance that your plan for me which demonstrates your love and mercy also includes those whom I love and hold dear. May my actions, deeds, words, and thoughts reflect your holy nature. May all that I do demonstrate your love to those with whom I interact this day.

When I fall short of your holiness, may I recognize my sin and come to you in humility and repentance with the knowledge that you will receive me, forgive me, and continue to love me.

May I walk in your ways, O God, trusting you, loving you, and serving those who come into my life this day.

In the name of Jesus, I pray. Amen.

> The Father's love shield me this day;
> The Son's pure wisdom cheer my way;
> The Holy Spirit's joy and light
> Drive from my heart the shades of night.[17]

...for the middle of the day

Loving God,

You invite your children to meet you every day in prayer. For some, that time occurs at the beginning of our day, early in the morning. During that time, we are able to thank you for keeping us through the previous night and to ask for your blessing upon our new day.

For others, prayer at the end of the day, prior to entering a time of sleep and refreshment, is when we talk with you and remember your blessings that have come to us throughout the day and evening hours.

Morning and evening…it is as if we "bookend" our day. But Lord, there are many times in our daily walk when we need to stop what we are doing during the middle of the day. We need a reminder of your presence. A situation may arise that requires your blessing and touch. Perhaps we simply need to pause and reconnect with you and thank you for what you have already done this day, and smile and rejoice in what you will continue to do before nightfall.

Dear Lord, I take this present moment to praise you and lift you up for what you have done and to give you thanks for what you will continue to reveal to me this day. I pray for your continued blessing and presence in the remainder of the day. I praise you, Lord, for who you are and for what you do in my life.

Thank you for always hearing my prayer. In Jesus' name, Amen.

> Be thou my vision, O Lord of my heart;
> Naught be all else to me, save that thou art:
> Thou my best thought both by day and by night,
> Waking or sleeping, thy presence my light.[18]

...for the end of the day

O Lord of Light,

The sun has set and the brightness that showered the earth this day has faded away. Yet the brightness of your presence and love continues to shine in my life as I come to the close of this day.

As I reflect back over the hours, I give you thanks for those moments that you have directed, the words of encouragement you have inspired me to speak, and the acts of mercy and love you have empowered me to share with others. I praise you for the many blessings I have received from you through the actions of others.

There have been occasions this day, Lord, where I have fallen short of your mark and what you would have had me do. I confess my sin to you, Lord. I specifically remember and confess _____ and _____. As I confess those sins of commission, I also confess my failure to do what I could have done for others but failed to do. Forgive me, Lord, I pray.

Now Father, I pray for your peace and protection through this coming night. May my sleep be restful, and may your holy angels keep watch over me.

I ask this in your name, the God who neither slumbers nor sleeps but always watches over me. Amen.

> Before the ending of the day,
> Creator of the world we pray!
> Thy grace and peace to us allow
> And be our guard and keeper now.[19]

...for strengthening my prayer time

Lord, teach me
   ...to treasure my prayer time with you.
Lord, teach me
   ...to think through my prayer time with you.
Lord, teach me
   ...to live my life as ongoing prayer time with you.
Lord, teach me
   ...to be bold and specific in my prayer time with you.
Lord, teach me
   ...to listen during my prayer time with you.
Lord, teach me
   ...to trust you during my prayer time with you.
Lord, teach me
   ...to pray.

> Come my soul, with ev'ry care,
> Jesus loves to answer prayer;
> He Himself has bid thee pray,
> Therefore will not turn away.[20]

...for a deeper relationship with God

O my Savior,

I pray for an ever-growing and deepening relationship with you. May the roots of my faith and dependence upon you become stronger and more firmly rooted in you day by day. I pray that I be not shaken by the storms and winds of distraction that could tempt me to retreat from reaching out to you and relying upon you every moment of each day.

May my day begin and end with you. May all the events and activities between the beginning and the end of the day be guided by you. May I rely solely upon you in all things, O Lord. May I come to the waters of your Living Word, day by day, to be strengthened and nourished. May my thoughts and plans be centered in you. May my actions, words, and deeds always reflect that I belong to you.

I pray in your holy name, O God, my Redeemer and Lord. Amen.

> Grant that I only You may love
> And seek those things which are above
> Till I behold You face to face,
> O Light eternal, through Your grace.[21]

...for the Spirit

Gracious Holy Spirit,

Be present and active in my daily walk. I thank you for and acknowledge your activity and power in my life by

...the gift of saving faith I have received.

...the words of grace and mercy I am able to speak to others.

...the deeds of kindness I am blessed and privileged to do for others.

...the spiritual, physical, and relational healing I experience from you.

...the joy and peace I have in knowing Jesus.

...the gratitude and thanks I am able to express to my Heavenly Father for his provisions and sustaining love in my life.

...the love that fills my heart for those who have been placed in my life.

...the words and actions of thanksgiving I am able to express for all the blessings in my life.

Come, Holy Spirit. Continue to dwell in my life. Fill me. Lead me. Nourish me each day of my life. May I walk with you always, I pray. Amen.

> Come down, O love divine; Seek Thou this soul of mine,
> And visit it with Thine own ardor glowing;
> O Comforter, draw near; Within my heart appear,
> And kindle it, Thy holy flame bestowing.[22]

...for my service to God

"O Jesus, I have promised to serve you to the end."

Lord, I sing those words. I speak those words. I pray those words. Then something occurs in my daily walk, and I forget those words. I become distracted and discouraged by certain events or by my sinful actions and thoughts. I take a detour from the path of "serving you to the end." Please forgive me, Lord.

When those times of distraction tempt me to stop serving you and, instead, start serving myself, may I remember how you have served me. You came into the world not to be served, but to be a servant to all of humankind.

May I model and follow your example of service and love. May I be empowered by your Holy Spirit to serve those whose lives cross my path and interact in my life as I proceed in the journey you have called me to follow. May my service to others be an image of the love and example you have already shown to me.

I love you, Lord. May I serve you and others in all that I think and say and do. In your holy name, I pray. Amen.

> O Jesus, I have promised to serve you to the end;
> Remain forever near me, my master and my friend.
> I shall not fear the battle if you are by my side,
> Nor wander from the pathway if you will be my guide.[23]

...for times of learning how to pray

Gracious Lord,
Teach me
...to treasure my prayer time with you.
Teach me
...to live my life as a time of ongoing prayer with you.
Teach me
...to think through my prayer time with you.
Teach me
...to come to you with trust during my prayer time with you.
Teach me
...to come with confidence during my prayer time with you.
Teach me
...to remove all doubts and fears during my prayer time with you.
Teach me
...to give thanks for all your blessings to me during my prayer time with you.
Teach me
...to know that you hear and answer my prayers according to your perfect and holy will.
In your holy name, Amen.

>   Amen, that is, so shall it be.
>   Make strong our faith in You, that we
>   May doubt not but with trust believe
>   That when we ask we shall receive.
>   Thus in Your name and at Your Word
>   We say, "Amen, O hear us, Lord!"[24]

... for seeking guidance and direction

Lord of my life,

You have assured me that you are my Good Shepherd. You have promised that you will guide and direct me throughout every situation in life that crosses my path and challenges me. Whether the challenge be physical, financial, emotional, relational, or spiritual, I know that you are close by and ready to lead me through any problems that come my way.

Dear Lord, I am facing one of those times right now. Specifically, I pray for your guidance and direction in the area(s) of _____.

I know that you have my welfare and future in your hand and that you will give me the peace and affirmation needed to bring me through this time of my life.

I trust you, God. You are faithful. You have shown your faithfulness to me again and again. I love you. I give every area of my life to you with confidence, knowing that you will direct your Holy Spirit to lead me and direct me in all of my actions and decisions.

Thank you, Lord, for being near to me, loving me, and hearing my prayer. Amen.

> I leave all things to God's direction;
> He loves me both in joy and woe.
> His will is good, sure His affection;
> His tender love is true, I know.
> My fortress and my rock is He;
> What pleases God, that pleases me.[25]

...for God's mercy

"Lord, have mercy. Christ, have mercy. Lord, have mercy."

Lord, this is a prayer that I need to pray every day. Sometimes I need to pray it more than once a day. Likely, I need to pray it every hour! The wonderful truth of this prayer is that you do have mercy. You show your mercy in a myriad of ways. Your love, your forgiveness, your provisions, your comfort, and your peace are just a few of the ways in which you share your mercy with me on my daily journey.

Lord, I thank you for your tender mercies to me. Without them, I would be lost as I travel each day through my life. May I always be mindful of how you care for me and give me exactly what I need in your unending compassion.

May my life demonstrate to others the gift of your mercy that fills my soul. Thank you, dear Lord, for your great love and mercy to me. Amen.

> O Lord, my God to Thee I pray:
> O cast me not in wrath away!
> Let Thy good Spirit ne'er depart,
> But let Him draw to Thee my heart
> That truly penitent I be:
> O God, be merciful to me![26]

...for times of discouragement

"Out of the depths I cry to you, O LORD. Lord, hear my voice!" (Ps. 130:1-2).

The valley of discouragement is not a place that I wish to occupy. It is a place that tries to pull me down. O Lord, I pray that you might reveal rays of encouragement that will erase the feelings of hopelessness that often try to hold me back from fulfilling the plans you have for me.

Dear God, I pray that your gift of encouragement would illuminate those times when I feel disappointment and doubt myself and the abilities you have given to me. May I live with the assurance that even when things don't go exactly the way I planned, there is always a better plan already in place for me.

May I recognize that discouragement is always a weapon of the enemy. Rather than spending time focusing on his attacks, I should always be mindful of all the good you have provided and will continue to provide for me.

You always want what is the very best for me, Lord. May I continually live in that truth even during those times when I am tempted to doubt and forget your promises. Your mercies and encouragement are new every day. Thank you for lifting me up and sustaining me throughout my life. Amen.

>Have we trials and temptations?
>Is there trouble anywhere?
>We should never be discouraged
>Take it to the Lord in prayer.
>Can we find a friend so faithful
>Who will all our sorrows share?
>Jesus knows our ev'ry weakness
>Take it to the Lord in prayer.[27]

...for God's forgiveness to me and others

Loving Father,

You give me the gift of your forgiveness when I come to you in faith, confess, and repent of my sin. Your mercy and love are given to me because of your Son, my Lord, Jesus Christ and what he has done for me on the cross. Thank you, Lord.

I pray, O God, that I might have a heart of mercy and love to freely forgive those who sin against me. As I travel on my daily journey, there will be times when I am wronged and hurt by the actions of others. In those times when it is hardest to forgive, may I remember and recall the gift of your forgiveness and love that you freely give to me. May my actions and response to those who sin against me be guided and inspired by what you have done for me and continue to do.

May I show the same grace and forgiveness to others that you show to me though your Son. May I never take your gift of forgiveness for granted. I ask this in the holy name of Jesus. Amen.

>I, a sinner, come to Thee
>With a penitent confession.
>Savior, mercy show to me;
>Grant for all my sins remission.
>Let these words my soul relieve:
>Jesus sinners doth receive.[28]

...*for times of thanksgiving*

"O give thanks to the LORD, for he is good, for his steadfast love endures forever" (Ps. 136:1). O Lord, this is a prayer I have prayed for as long as I can remember. It is a prayer that passes easily over my lips. It comes to mind so easily that I can speak the words without taking the time to meditate upon them and contemplate how meaningful they can be.

Forgive me, Lord, for speaking these words without praying them. You have given me all that I possess. Help me, dear God, to express my gratitude and thanks to you for your mercy and love, your faithfulness and provision, my family and friends, my health and home, my employment and education, and, most importantly, the gift of salvation that you have given to me through the merits of your Son, my Savior, Jesus.

May I worship and praise you as a response for what you have freely given to me. May I give you my unending thanks for all you have done and continue to do in my life.

I pray in the name of Jesus. Amen.

> Praise, my soul, the King of heaven;
> To His feet your tribute bring;
> Ransomed, healed, restored, forgiven,
> Evermore His praises sing:
> Alleluia, alleluia!
> Praise the everlasting King.[29]

... for dealing with relationships

Father in Heaven,

You have created the human race to be in relationship. We interact with parents, children, siblings, spouses, other family members, colleagues, and casual acquaintances every day of our life. Having people in our life who support us, love us, and come alongside of us in both difficult times and in times of joy is one of the many blessings we experience in our journey of life. I thank you, Lord, for those individuals you have placed in my life who bless and love me with their presence and support.

There can also be times when relationships with others are tested, strained, and occasionally broken because of our sinful pride, our self-interests, and misunderstandings. Sometimes we fail to communicate or we hesitate to admit our own faults in contributing to a broken relationship or friendship.

Heavenly Father, I confess that there are times when I allow my sin and self-centeredness to get in the way of rebuilding and restoring a healthy Christ-centered relationship with another person. Lord, when I behave in that manner, please forgive me.

I give you thanks and praise for those areas of my life that you bless with special friendships and relationships. May I always express my gratitude to you and to those whom you have placed in my life. In Jesus' most holy name, I pray. Amen.

> Lord of all nations, grant me grace
> To love all people, ev'ry race;
> And in each person may I see
> My kindred, loved, redeemed by Thee.[30]

... for times of unexpected testing

Heavenly Father,

Life is full of unexpected surprises—some joyous and others unwanted, discouraging, and painful. It is often during the aftermath of these surprises that unwelcome outcomes appear and bring experiences and testing that potentially lead us to the point of breaking. A medical diagnosis that comes without warning, the revelation of an unfaithful spouse, the ongoing marathon of a rebellious child, false accusations against us—a list like this can test our faith and confidence, and overwhelm us.

Lord, it is during those difficult times that we need to be especially reminded of your faithfulness, your divine providence, your love, and your care for us. Even as the enemy would make every attempt to bring us down, may we be constantly mindful that "the one who is in you is greater than the one who is in the world" (1 John 4:4). While the enemy's greatest weapon is discouragement, I need not worry. My faith and foundation are fixed in you.

May I never falter in trusting you and placing my complete confidence in your love and salvation. May the words of your prophet always be in my mind and heart as you share the "future with hope" (Jer. 29:11) that you have planned for me.

Thank you, Lord, for your love and encouragement and faithfulness to me. Amen.

> Fear not! I am with you, O be not dismayed,
> For I am your God and will still give you aid;
> I'll strengthen you, help you, and cause you to stand,
> Upheld by My righteous omnipotent hand[31]

... *for discernment in a time of transition*

Loving Shepherd of the sheep,

I come to you as one who is facing a time of change and transition in my life. What was comfortable and familiar is no longer a part of my life. I am in a time of wandering, wondering what the future holds for me in a new setting. It's almost as though I am like a lost sheep that is uncertain which direction to take.

I have different options from which to choose. Some of them are clearer than others. As I move from the known to the unknown, I pray for your guidance and direction. You are my Good Shepherd. I humbly ask you to guide me with your love and protection. Please give me the wisdom and discernment that I need to help me through this time of uncertainty.

I love you, Lord Jesus. I trust you. May I follow you in all of my ways. In your name, I pray. Amen.

> The King of love my shepherd is,
> Whose goodness faileth never;
> I nothing lack if I am His
> And He is mine forever.[32]

...for facing an unexpected medical diagnosis

Lord God, healer of my soul,

I have been diagnosed with a medical condition that is unexpected. My physician has informed me that I am facing _____. Obviously, I would rather not have to deal with this condition. However, the reality is that I *am* facing it.

Dear Lord, I know that I am in your hands. You are the Great Physician. You have already given me the greatest healing there is: the forgiveness of my sin. I praise you and thank you for that healing, Lord.

Now, I humbly and confidently ask you to touch and heal a different area of my life. I pray for the healing of my body and the restoration of my health.

As I go through the days that lie before me, please continue to give me your peace and the assurance of your healing presence in my life. In all things I trust you, Father, for your perfect will for me. Great Physician, I believe that you will touch me and care for me in a way that brings glory to you and peace to my soul.

Thank you, Lord, for loving me and caring for me. Amen.

> O be our great deliv'rer still,
> The Lord of life and death;
> Restore and quicken, soothe and bless,
> With Your life-giving breath.
> To hands that work and eyes that see
> Give wisdom's healing pow'r
> That whole and sick and weak and strong
> May praise You evermore.[33]

... for dealing with the death of a loved one

O God of mercy and love,

Dealing with the death of a loved one is not easy. We think about the fact that we will not see a certain person on this earth again. While we look forward to the heavenly reunion we will have with those whom we love and have died in Jesus, it is, nevertheless, still a time of sorrow.

Lord, I am thinking about and remembering _____ who recently died. I loved and cared about _____ very much. Please give me your comfort and peace. May I trust in your promise of the Resurrection and remember that you have prepared a place for all of your children.

While I mourn the death of my loved one, may I, at the same time, live with confidence and assurance of your peace. Thank you, Lord, for your great mercy for me as I mourn. You bring consolation and hope. I praise and trust you and give you thanks for your mercy and love to me.

I pray this prayer in your holy name—Father, Son, and Holy Spirit. Amen.

> When peace, like a river, attendeth my way;
> When sorrows, like sea billows, roll;
> Whatever my lot, Thou hast taught me to say,
> It is well, it is well with my soul.
> It is well with my soul,
> It is well, it is well with my soul.[34]

... for the birth of a child or grandchild

O Creator of Life,

I praise your name and give thanks for the birth of _____, a blessing who brings me great joy and happiness. I pray that you would send your holy angels to guard and protect this little child as she continues to grow.

I pray, also, that you would surround _____ with people who will love and care for her and also model and share the love of Jesus.

May this infant grow in knowledge of and love for you as she goes through life. May _____ walk with you and learn your ways. May she learn to know the love of Jesus. May she always know your presence and love in her life.

Thank you for your blessing to me to be a part of this child's life. I pray for your wisdom as I love this baby and help her to know you.

In your holy name, I pray. Amen.

> Jesus loves me! This I know,
> For the Bible tells me so.
> Little ones to Him belong;
> They are weak, but He is strong.
> Yes, Jesus loves me! Yes, Jesus loves me!
> Yes, Jesus loves me! The Bible tells me so.[35]

...for God's benefits to me

O Lord, the psalmist writes, "Bless the LORD, O my soul, and do not forget all his benefits" (Ps. 103:2).

I bless you, Lord, for your forgiveness of my sin.
Blessed be your name, dear Lord.

I bless you, Lord, for your healing of my diseases.
Blessed be your name, dear Lord.

I bless you, Lord, for your deliverance of my spirit from the pit of discouragement.
Blessed be your name, dear Lord.

I bless you, Lord, for crowning me with never-ending love and mercy.
Blessed be your name, dear Lord.

I bless you, Lord, for satisfying me with all that is good.
Blessed be your name, O Lord.

I bless you, Lord, for your compassion and care for me.
Blessed be your name, O Lord.

"Bless the LORD, O my soul" (Ps. 103:2). Eternal praise and adoration be to you—Father, Son, and Holy Spirit. Amen.

> Praise to the Lord! O let all that is in me adore Him!
> All that has life and breath, come now with praises before Him!
> Let the Amen sound from His people again;
> Gladly forever adore Him![36]

...for my child

Heavenly Father,

    I come to you as one to whom you have given the gift of a child. I thank you, dear Lord, for the gift of parenthood I have received. I recognize this tremendous responsibility. I pray that I might be a parent who reflects your image and love to my son. I pray that you would give me wisdom and patience in raising my child in the love of Jesus.

    At the same time, Lord, I want to pray for _____ (name). Growing up in today's world is not easy. Peer pressure, temptations, and the influence of this world are always present. Unfortunately, those elements are not always representative of your will and ways. I pray that my son would always know that Jesus is his Savior and best friend. When he faces challenges and difficult questions, may he always remember that Jesus is with him and that he can come to me for support and love.

    May the wisdom and gift of faith that you have given to me always be evident to share with and help guide my child. May my life always be one that shows the love of Jesus and encourages _____ (name). I pray that you would always protect, guard, and keep him close to you.

    I pray in your loving Son's name, Jesus Christ. Amen.

> Let children hear the mighty deeds
> Which God performed of old,
> Which in our younger days we saw,
> And which our parents told.
>
> To learn that in our God alone
> Their hope securely stands,
> That they may never doubt his love
> But walk in His commands.[37]

... for times when life isn't fair

Loving Father, Gracious God,

I confess to you that there are times in my life when I look at the world and say to myself, "Life isn't fair!" Most of the time my complaint is a result of self-pity and when I am feeling sorry for myself. I fail to remember how blessed I am. I think about things I don't have rather than everything you have given to me.

At other times I see individuals rewarded for an "average" effort, while my work and effort are not acknowledged. Again, I think to myself, "Life isn't fair!"

Lord, this attitude is not pleasing to you. It is self-centered, selfish, and ungrateful. It is sinful. I confess my sin, repent of it, and humbly ask for your forgiveness.

I pray that you will give me a heart of humility and generosity. Never allow a spirit of jealousy to be present in my spirit. Give me an attitude of joy that allows me to rejoice with others when they receive a blessing or acknowledgement for a job well done.

Most of all, Lord, I thank you that despite my sin, you love me and sent Jesus to save me. You have gone beyond being "fair" and have given me the gift of eternal life. Thank you, Lord. In your name, I pray. Amen.

> O my Savior, help afford
> By Your Spirit and Your Word!
> When my wayward heart would stray,
> Keep me in the narrow way;
> Grace in time of need supply
> While I live and when I die.[38]

... for protection against the devil

Mighty God,

Satan seeks to attack, assault, and devour your children. He is always on the prowl (1 Pet. 5:8). He will use any means he can to wage spiritual war against your flock. But all praise and thanks be to you—Father, Son, and Holy Spirit.

You are a mighty fortress (Ps. 91:2).

You are my rock and salvation (Ps. 62:2).

You are the cornerstone (Eph. 2:20).

You are the Good Shepherd of the sheep (Ps. 23:1).

You are my Redeemer (Isa. 44:6).

You are my hiding place and shield (Ps. 119:114).

You are my Savior (Isa. 43:11).

Mighty God,

I place myself in your care. I pray that you would keep a hedge of protection around me and spare me from all of Satan's schemes. I put my full faith and trust in you, dear Lord. You are my God and I commend myself to your loving mercy. In your powerful name, I pray. Amen.

> Though devils all the world should fill,
> All eager to devour us,
> We tremble not, we fear no ill;
> They shall not over-pow'r us.
> This world's prince may still
> Scowl fierce as he will,
> He can harm us none.
> He's judged; the deed is done;
> One little word can fell him.[39]

...for God-pleasing decisions

Father, Son, and Holy Spirit,

As I walk through this life, I encounter many crossroads requiring me to make a decision. Sometimes the decisions are obvious. I am able to consider all of the possibilities and select the answer that rises above all of the others. On some occasions there are a variety of answers that are all positive. Any of the answers would be a good decision.

Then, however, there are those times that present options when none of the answers stand out above the others. Perhaps it is because I have a "blind spot." It may be because I am not listening to your voice. Possibly it is because I have a predetermined answer in my mind that ignores an obvious answer from you, but I exercise a spirit of rebellion or independence that is not in agreement with your will.

Dear God, I humbly pray that I might always be in relationship with you and seeking your wisdom and guidance for decisions that are in keeping with your will for my life. May all of my decisions, large and small, be in agreement with your plan for me.

In your holy name, I pray. Amen.

> Grant me the strength to do
> With ready heart and willing
> Whatever You command,
> My calling here fulfilling;
> That I do what I should
> While trusting You to bless
> The outcome for my good,
> For You must give success.[40]

... for trusting God's will

My Lord and God,

The Scriptures instruct us to trust in you with our whole heart and not lean on our own understanding (Prov. 3:5). You have shown time and time again in my lifetime and in the lives of others that you are trustworthy.

There are times, however, when, like the children of Israel, I doubt you and your will. Forgive me, Lord. I am sorry for my unbelief.

May I always walk through my journey in life believing and knowing that I can trust you and your will for my life.

You have never failed me. You are trustworthy even when I fail you. Your will and plan for me are perfect and holy.

In those times when my trust and faith in you falter, please strengthen me with the gift of your Holy Spirit.

I pray, trusting you and your will for me. Amen.

> The will of God is always best
> And shall be done forever;
> And they who trust in Him are blest;
> He will forsake them never.
> He helps indeed
> In time of need;
> He chastens with forbearing.
> They who depend on God their friend,
> Shall not be left despairing.[41]

...for being a "voice" for God

Dear Heavenly Father,

Throughout history you have spoken your will and plan of salvation through the words of your prophets, the writers of Scripture, and your messengers of the gospel. Your message of hope has been heard by millions of your children from the beginning of time to the present day. The world still needs to hear the story of Jesus and his love. Many of your sons and daughters live in darkness. They have not heard the "Good News."

Lord God, I pray that I can share your Word. I pray that I might be one of the many who proclaim the wonderful story of Jesus and how he changes lives. I have many close friends and some family members who do not know your Son and his love.

There are times when I hesitate to speak. Sometimes my words lack the power that your Holy Spirit can give. Lord, today I pray for that power. I pray that I might be a messenger for you in the world where I live every day.

The opportunities to share the gospel are never-ending. May I be a voice who shares that message. In your holy name, I pray. Amen.

> Oh, for a thousand tongues to sing
> My great Redeemer's praise,
> The glories of my God and King,
> The triumphs of His grace!
>
> My gracious Master and my God,
> Assist me to proclaim,
> To spread through all the earth abroad,
> The honors of Thy name.[42]

Part 3

Poems for the Daily Walk

We Run the Race

... let us run with perseverance the race ...
(Heb. 12:1)

We run the race with eyes fixed high.
Our Lord's example testifies
That those who listen to his call
Will persevere into "Faith's Hall."

With mercy, God, you show us how to be your people here
On earth to do the task you give with kindness and no fear.
The hindrances and obstacles of roadblocks on the way
Will not deter the path for us: your plan we will obey.

We run the race with eyes fixed high.
Our Lord's example testifies
That those who listen to his call
Will persevere into "Faith's Hall."

The years have been a testament to Christ's unfailing grace.
Though times of doubt and sorrow appear, he's always in his place
Beside the Father, loving us with those who ran the race.
They did not stop, did not retreat until they saw his face.

We run the race with eyes fixed high.
Our Lord's example testifies
That those who listen to his call
Will persevere into "Faith's Hall."

So on this day our praises soar with alleluias loud.
The time is now, the place is here amidst a needy crowd
Of those who seek the Savior's love and long to know "The Way."
We move ahead, we stay the course, we go without delay.

We run the race with eyes fixed high.
Our Lord's example testifies
That those who listen to his call
Will persevere into "Faith's Hall."

Holy Hearts, Holy Minds

*... whatever is true, whatever is honorable, whatever is just,
whatever is pure, whatever is pleasing, whatever is commendable ...*
(Phil. 4:8)

The thoughts that we create each day
Reflect our inner part.
The thinking of our minds and hearts
Are never far apart.
What comes from deep inside of us
Shows who we really are.
We pray for messages from God
To share both near and far.

These messages of purity
Reveal the Lord within
Each one of us who love him so
Yet daily battle sin.
We aren't alone, we carry on.
We're loved in God's own tether.
We know that holy hearts and minds
Are gifts from him forever.

Delight Yourself, Commit Your Way

Take delight ... Commit your way
(Ps. 37:4-5)

Delight yourself, commit your way is what we're called to do.
Those simple words describe a path that helps to see us through
To peace and joy, God's love and grace, his action and deep caring.
He's always present in our life, his mercy ever sharing.

We sometimes fail to follow ways our loving Lord provides.
And when we don't, we often fall along the path of pride.
Those bumps can be discouraging and cause us pain and grief.
In times like that we wonder if we'll ever know relief.

Despite our independence and thinking we know best,
Our heavenly Father stays close by to give his peaceful rest.
To his dear children near and far, to all who call him Lord,
He guides, encourages, and shows the way—all gifts that he affords.

Praise God, the Father, Son, and Spirit who lead us on our journey.
Take your delight, commit your way, and always be discerning.
To listen for the voice of One whose Word is always true.
We trust, we follow, we give our all to the Lord who makes all things new.

Walking Away

Trust in the LORD with all your heart, and do not rely on your own insight.
(Prov. 3:5)

Walking away when it's hard to do is something people face.
It usually happens to most of us when we find we're out of place.
Sometimes we'll stumble in the dark before we know to leave.
Because there are some messages we choose not to believe.

Some others often fail to leave when everything is clear.
They hesitate and make excuses e'en when they ought to fear
The consequence of choices made that leads to hurt and pain
Instead of following the road that gives them hope again.

It's ne'er too late to do the thing that for each one is best.
Reach out in faith and ask the Lord to show his way to rest.
And when he tells you what to do, have trust and show no fear.
For in your heart, and soul, and life, you'll know he's always near.

When to Leave

For everything there is a season, and a time for every matter under heaven.
(Eccl. 3:1)

You know it's time to leave when
... people don't look you in the eye.

... people say, "Let's get together," but aren't available to meet with you.

... people leave notes rather than speak with you face to face.

... you know that no matter what you do, things won't change.

... people don't talk with you; they talk about you.

... you are perceived as part of the problem instead of part of the solution.

... others see you as a threat, not an ally.

... you are described as an obstacle, not an enabler.

... people "beat around the bush" rather than come to the point.

... joy is replaced by frustration and disappointment.

... God calls you to something else.

When God Says "Go"

Go from your country ...
(Gen. 12:1)

When God says "Go," he lets us know
    by showing us a new way.

He speaks to those whose hearts he knows
    will welcome yet a new day.

Oft times the voice is very soft;
    it can be hard to hear.

Especially if we're turned within
    and don't give him our ear.

But if we give him all we are,
    our hopes, desires, and dreams,

He'll show us how to move in life
    and come to living streams.

When God says "Go," you take his hand
    and let him guide you clearly.

By trusting him and following him
    you'll find he loves you dearly.

New Beginnings

See, I am making all things new.
(Rev. 21:5)

New beginnings allow us to

... catch our breath.

... let go of things that hold us back.

... stop and give thanks for the past.

... dream new dreams.

... reestablish our priorities.

... recommit ourselves to those things that matter.

... exercise our faith.

... refocus our energy.

... trust God in a whole new way.

... see what surprises God may have for us.

... come to a new understanding of God's call.

... move in new directions.

... write new chapters.

... pray new prayers.

... rejoice in God's faithfulness and promises.

My Time on Earth

So teach us to count our days ...
(Ps. 90:12)

My time on earth is short, decreasing day by day.
I have no way to lengthen it, no matter come what may.
I only have from now to then when my brief life will cease.
My prayer is that I follow Christ and live my days in peace.

There is no better way to live; all other paths are haunted.
I travel on the road he gave with confidence undaunted.
And while the time that yet remains grows briefer hour by hour.
I move with eyes fixed on the one who sends the Spirit's power.

And as I run with open eyes fixed on the goal before,
It comes more clear every day I'm closer to the shore.
And with the time I yet possess I long to live for him,
So others' lives will be blessed by my deeds from within.

O Morning Sun

Keep awake therefore, for you do not know on what day your Lord is coming.
(Matt. 24:42)

O morning sun, O morning sun, you beckon us to rise
And shed the cloak of night's dark veil and welcome God's new prize.
We look not back nor gaze ahead. We only ponder now.
We think not 'bout the tasks before. The Lord will show us how.

The morning sun, the morning sun, moves up into the sky
To light the day and meet the birds who whistle as they fly.
But what of us? How do we spend the time that we've received?
We dare not let it slip away lest we become deceived.

Deceived, you say? That cannot be! Yet we must be beware.
The sun is through the noonday hour and we have yet to share
The love of Jesus for the world whom he himself has saved
To bring us to himself in heaven his life for all he gave.

The morning sun, the morning sun, is setting in the west.
Its rays are gradually dimming as it finds a place to rest.
Before the final darkness descends upon us all,
Take one last opportunity to heed the Savior's call.

O morning sun, O morning sun, you beckon us to rise
And take the love of Jesus and declare it to the skies.
We may not tell it perfectly or fill the fisher's net.
But we can do our part to share before the sun has set.

A Lasting Friendship

... I have called you friends ...
(John 15:15)

Jesus gives a friendship, free, an oasis on life's journey,
A place where you can always be with One who's ever serving.
It's where you go to seek and find the kindred Spirit's presence.
It's where you rest when others flee and leave you without hope.

Jesus is the Living Stream amid life's arid desert,
A friend whose judgment is never passed nor condemnation given.
You meet with him, you share your cares that mark your deepest feelings.
He's always near, not far away; his love he's always sharing.

Lord Jesus is the Solid Rock. He always will support you.
He will not shift amidst the tide that seeks to overwhelm you.
Upon him you can always rest your heart, and soul, and sorrows.
His friendship lasts not only now, but all of life's tomorrows.

When Others Let You Down

But he denied it, saying, "Woman, I do not know him."
(Luke 22:57)

What can you say? What can you do,
    when others let you down?
The ones you think you know the best
    oft make a choice that's bound
    to be the "easiest" way to go
    regardless of the cost,
    instead of staying close to you
    and living out "the cross."

The choices that matter in this life
    are really very few.
So when those choices come to you,
    it matters what you do.
To be a faithful friend to one
    amidst a time of need
    is better than to walk away
    and think your conscience freed.

I cannot tell you what to do.
I hope that you will know,
    that faithfulness and loyalty
    are traits the Lord bestows
    to all his children, devoted friends,
    who know the gospel way
    and now can make a choice that shows
    his love to all, I pray.

The People of the Lord

And let us consider how to provoke one another to love and good deeds,
not neglecting to meet together ...
(Heb. 10:24-25)

The people of the Lord have gathered in this place,
    to hear him speak to all through word and song.
The message he has is one of hope and love,
    a touch of Jesus' presence e'er so strong.

Our backgrounds are diverse from every walk of life,
    a blessing that can help us reach the lost.
We strive to follow Christ and heed the Savior's call,
    to love the world no matter what the cost.

The blending of our lives from near and far away,
    displays the love of God that makes us one.
We share our common thoughts, our needs, our prayers, our wants:
    this helps us finish races we all run.

We thank God for this gift of grace so undeserved,
    that feeds our weary spirits in this place.
Our hearts we give, O Lord, to serve you with our lives,
    until we stand before you face to face.

Counting the Cost

For which of you, intending to build a tower,
does not first sit down and estimate the cost ...
(Luke 14:28)

To build a tower, you need to plan
    and gather information.
You look at facts and figures, too,
    as part of preparation.
There's much to do; it takes great time
    to complete the task at hand.
But when you finish all the work,
    your tower before you stands.

Our Lord and Master speaks words to us
    that ask us to count the cost.
He shares a picture with each of us
    as well as with "the lost."
To be a follower of him
    requires all we are.
Without his vision that's clear and plain,
    we will not travel far.

The road is rough, requiring much
    to see our travel through.
But counting up the cost it takes
    is something we can do.
And as we count, we can be sure
    the Savior will provide.
He's walked the path; he's paid the price;
    he's always by our side.

The Mind of Christ

Let the same mind be in you that was in Christ Jesus ...
(Phil. 2:5)

What are the thoughts within our minds?
What values fill our hearts?
What visions occupy that space
Where ideas have their starts?

Does what's inside convey the way
That Jesus showed on Earth
To live and die in humbleness?
His love shows us our worth.

The way he lived while on this orb
Was different than we live.
He gave up everything he had,
Eternal life to give.

The need that led him to this place
Was prompted by "The Fall."
His way of thinking led him to say,
"I'll give my life for all."

The mind of Christ is God's wish for us
He asks us to receive,
The peace and joy that Jesus gives
To all who will believe.

The mind of Christ that fills our minds
Will guide us day by day.
The way of Jesus will not fail.
From him we will not stray.

My Lord and God

My Lord and my God!
(John 20:28)

My Lord and God, I worship you
And lift your name on high.
I praise you for your majesty
And proclaim it to the sky.
You reign supreme, above all things.
No limits hold you in.
Your gift for me has always been
Your gift that conquered sin.

My Lord and God, I pray to you.
On bended knee I bow
My head and heart before your throne
To offer you my vow.
A promise that conveys my wish
To follow in your ways.
Your loving plan designed for me
I'll follow all my days.

My Lord and God, I close my lips
And listen with my ears
The quiet words you speak to me
To silence all my fears.
I hear your voice amidst the stillness
Of your eternal love.
Your messages of calm and peace
Are sent from heaven above.

My Lord and God, I give you thanks
For watching over me
And giving me eternal life.
Your gift has made me free.
I love you, Lord. I give my all.
I want to live for you.
My heart is yours. I'll follow you
Each day my whole life through.

Notes

1 Dallas Willard, *Hearing God: Developing a Conversational Relationship with God* (Downers Grove: InterVarsity Press, 1999), 200.
2 Oswald Chambers, *My Utmost for His Highest* (Uhrichville, OH: Barbour Books, 1963), August 2.
3 Henry W. Baker, "The King of Love, My Shepherd Is," (No. 709) in *Lutheran Service Book: Pew Edition* (St. Louis: Concordia Publishing House, 2006) [hereafter *LSB*].
4 Chambers, March 17.
5 Henri Nouwen, *With Open Hands* (New York: Random House Publishing Group, 1972), 3.
6 Martin Luther, "The Small Catechism," in *LSB*, 322
7 Frances R. Havergal, "Take My Life and Let it Be," (No. 783) in *LSB*.
8 Glenn Packiam, "Forseeing the Future: Confronting Our Focus on the Here and Now," *Worship Leader Magazine* 29, no. 23 (Sept. 2, 2020), https://worshipleader.com/leadership/worship-theology/foretasting-the-future-confronting-our-focus-on-the-here-and-now/.
9 Luther, 324.
10 Ibid
11 John Baille, *A Diary of Private Prayer*, rev. ed. (New York: Scribner, 1977), 91.
12 Edward Mote, "My Hope Is Built on Nothing Less," (No. 575) in *LSB*.
13 Baille, 63.
14 Sydney J. Harris, *Winners and Losers* (Niles, IL: Agnus Communications, 1968), 7.
15 Ibid., 17.
16 Frances Havergal, "I Am Trusting Thee, Lord Jesus," (No. 729) in *LSB*.
17 Martin Behm, trans. Conrad H. L. Schuette, "O Blessed Holy Trinity," (No. 876) in *LSB*.
18 Eleanor H. Hull, trans. Mary E. Byrne, "Be Thou My Vision," (No. 793) in *Evangelical Lutheran Worship: Pew Edition* (Minneapolis: Augsburg Fortress, 2006).
19 Latin 5th-10th cent., trans. John Mason Neale, "Before the Ending of the Day," (No. 889) in *LSB*.
20 John Newton, "Come, My Soul, with Every Care," (No. 779) in *LSB*.
21 Johann Friedrich Ruopp, trans. August Crull, "Renew Me, O Eternal Light," (No. 704) in *LSB*.
22 Bianco da Siena, trans. Richard F. Littledale, "Come Down, O Love Divine," (No. 501) in *LSB*.
23 John E. Bode, "O Jesus, I Have Promised," (No. 810) in *Evangelical Lutheran Worship: Pew Edition* (Minneapolis: Augsburg Fortress, 2006).
24 Martin Luther, trans. *The Lutheran Hymnal 1941*, "Our Father, Who from Heaven Above," (No. 766) in *LSB*.
25 Salomo Franck, trans. August Crull, "I Leave All Things to God's Direction," (No. 719) in *LSB*.
26 Magnus Brostrup Landstad, trans. Carl Döving, "To Thee, Omniscient Lord of All," (No. 613) in *LSB*.
27 Joseph M. Scriven, "What a Friend We Have in Jesus," (No. 770) in *LSB*.
28 Erdmann Neumeister, trans. *The Lutheran Hymnal 1941*, "Jesus Sinners Doth Receive," (No. 609) in *LSB*.
29 Henry F. Lyte, "Praise, My Soul, the King of Heaven, (No. 793) in *LSB*.
30 Olive Wise Spannaus, "Lord of All Nations, Grant Me Grace," (No. 844) in *LSB*.
31 *A Selection of Hymns*, London, 1787, "How Firm a Foundation," (No. 728) in *LSB*.
32 Henry W. Baker, "The King of Love My Shepherd Is," (No. 709) in *LSB*.
33 Edward H. Plumptre, "Your Hand, O Lord, in Days of Old," (No. 846) in *LSB*.
34 Horatio G. Spafford, "When Peace, Like a River, (No. 763) in *LSB*.
35 Anna B. Warner, "Jesus Loves Me," (No. 588) in *LSB*.
36 Joachim Neander, trans. Catherine Winkworth, "Praise to the Lord, the Almighty," (No.790) in *LSB*.
37 Isaac Watts, "Let Children Hear the Mighty Deeds," (No. 867) in *LSB*.
38 William McComb, "Chief of Sinners Though I Be," (No. 611) in *LSB*.
39 Martin Luther, "A Mighty Fortress is Our God," (No. 656) in *LSB*.
40 Johann Heerman, trans. Catherine Winkworth, "O God, My Faithful God," (No. 696) in *LSB*.
41 Albrecht von Preussen, trans. *The Lutheran Hymnal 1941*, "The Will of God is Always Best," (No. 758) in *LSB*.
42 Charles Wesley, "Oh, for a Thousand Tongues to Sing," (No. 528) in *LSB*.

Scripture Index

Genesis
3:15
 The Gift of "Do-Overs" 14
12:1
 A New Beginning 27
 When God Says "Go" 65

Exodus
4:20
 A New Beginning 27

Ruth
4:13
 A New Beginning 27

2 Samuel
12:13
 The Gift of "Do-Overs" 14

1 Kings
19:1-10
 Recognizing God's Vision 12

Psalms
23:1
 ...for protection against the devil 55
34:19
 The Vicissitudes of Life 25
36:5
 Living in the Clouds 24
37:4-5
 Delight Yourself, Commit Your Way 62
46:10
 This Is the Day 2
62:2
 ...for protection against the devil 55
86:5
 Let God Love You 18
86:11
 Following the Truth 7
90:12
 Counting the Days 4
 My Time on Earth 67
91:2
 ...for protection against the devil 55
103:2
 ...for God's benefits to me 52
118:24
 This Is the Day 2
119:114
 ...for protection against the devil 55
121:1
 The "Eyes" Have It 13
123:1-2
 The "Eyes" Have It 13
130:1-2
 ...for times of discouragement 43
136:1
 ...for times of thanksgiving 45

139:7-10
 Never Far Away 21

Proverbs
3:5
 ...for trusting God's will 57
 Walking Away 63
4:5
 Counting the Days 4
23:26
 The "Eyes" Have It 13

Ecclesiastes
3:1
 When to Leave 64

Isaiah
43:1
 Walking in God's Call 8
43:11
 ...for protection against the devil 55
43:18-19
 A New Beginning 27
44:6
 ...for protection against the devil 55

Jeremiah
29:11
 Recognizing God's Vision 12
 ...for times of unexpected testing 47
29:13
 Let God Love You 18

Lamentations
3:22-23
 The Seasons of Life 3

Jonah
3:1
 Obeying God's Voice 16

Matthew
4:1-11
 Temptations: We All Have Them 15
5:9
 Givers of Peace 28
8:23-27
 Wide Seas, Small Boats 22
11:28
 Let God Love You 18
 Words of Invitation 26
14:23
 Praying When No One Is Watching 9
24:42
 O Morning Sun 68
28:20
 Never Far Away 21

Luke
4:1-13
 Temptations: We All Have Them 15

14:28
 Counting the Cost 72
22:57
 When Others Let You Down 70
John
3:16
 Let God Love You 18
14:6
 Knowing the Way 5
14:27
 Givers of Peace 28
15:15
 A Lasting Friendship 69
17:17
 Following the Truth 7
20:19
 Unexpected Surprises 20
20:21
 Givers of Peace 28
20:26
 Givers of Peace 28
20:28
 My Lord and God 74
21:15-17
 The Gift of "Do-Overs" 14
Acts
9:1-9
 Recognizing God's Vision 12
9:4
 A New Beginning 27
16:25
 Always Keep on Singing 11
26:19
 Recognizing God's Vision 12
Romans
8:26
 Following the Truth 7
1 Corinthians
13:4-6
 The Greatest Thing 19
13:13
 The Greatest Thing 19
2 Corinthians
5:7
 Faith Walking 6
 The Vicissitudes of Life 25
Ephesians
1:18
 The "Eyes" Have It 13
2:20
 ...for protection against the devil 55
4:1
 Walking in God's Call 8
5:1-2
 Imitating God 29

Phillippians
2:5
 The Mind of Christ 73
4:8
 Holy Hearts, Holy Minds 61
Colossians
3:2
 Where Are Your Thoughts? 17
3:16
 Introduction xiii
2 Timothy
1:7
 Let God Love You 18
3:15
 Counting the Days 4
Hebrews
2:10
 Wide Seas, Small Boats 22
4:15
 Temptations: We All Have Them 15
10:24-25
 The People of the Lord 71
11:8
 Faith Walking 6
 A New Beginning 27
12:1
 We Run the Race 60
12:1-2
 Recognizing God's Vision 12
1 John
1:5-7
 The Greatest Thing 19
4:4
 ...for times of unexpected testing 47
4:7
 Imitating God 29
4:7-8
 The Greatest Thing 19
4:11
 Imitating God 29
4:16
 Let God Love You 18
5:4
 Winners and Losers 23
1 Peter
4:10
 Taking Care of God's Gifts 10
5:8
 ...for protection against the devil 55
Revelation
21:5
 New Beginnings 66